Faith and the Mystery of God

Faith and the Mystery of God

MAURICE WILES

Fortress Press   Philadelphia

First published in Great Britain by
SCM Press Ltd 1982

First Fortress Press edition 1982

Library of Congress Cataloging in Publication Data

Wiles, Maurice F.
Faith and the Mystery of God

Includes indexes.
1. Apologetics—20th century. I. Title.
BT1102.W525 1982   230   82-2451
ISBN 0-8006-1651-0   AACR2

9603D82   Printed in the United States of America   1-1651

CONTENTS

PREFACE

In *The Remaking of Christian Doctrine* (SCM Press 1974) I
attempted a critical discussion of some of the central facets of
traditional Christian doctrine. To some Christians that aim in
itself seemed suspect. But many scholars who had no complaints
to raise about the general aim were unhappy about the outcome.
It appeared to them to be 'negative' or 'unconstructive', failing
to do justice to the living character of Christian faith. That
criterion is one which I explicitly accept within the book itself
as appropriate to the assessment of a treatment of Christian
doctrine (pp. 108, 115). But that book had a limited role in that
respect. I described it as an attempt to clarify 'the basic framework within which we have to work' and spoke of the need for
'further work of a more tentative kind still to be done' (p. 120).
But the problem of how that further work is to be done, how to
spell out more fully and more richly the experienced content of
Christian belief, is an acute one. We live in an age which fosters
the critical intellect more than the creative imagination. Philosophically and culturally it is a fragmented age, so that what
speaks powerfully to one group of people may say little of
moment to others. Increasingly it has come to seem to me that
the creative expression of Christian faith today calls more for
the prophet in the face of particular situations than for the
theologian in his study. Yet the critical theologian still has a
role to play and he can justly be called upon to show the inter-

relation of his critical studies and the faith as it is believed and practised. But how can he do it responsibly in an age where we are so aware of the varieties both of imagery and of forms of faith?

The answer has seemed to me to write more personally about Christian faith, as I apprehend it, than I would naturally have chosen to do. I have tried not merely to describe that faith, but to give some account of the grounds for my holding it. It is my hope that the way in which it is presented here may prove of some help to others who are faced with the same problems. Despite the more personal approach, the book is still intended as a contribution to theology rather than as a piece of directly religious writing. I believe it to be consistent with my earlier writings and, as evidence of this, have included cross-references to those earlier works at various places in the notes. Whether the result embodies that more 'positive' or 'constructive' approach that some of my critics have desiderated, I must leave to others to judge.

I

On Being a Christian Today

Why am I a Christian? Many factors have combined to produce that result. Of some of them I am no doubt only dimly aware, if indeed I am conscious of them at all. But among those which are clear to me, one seems to be basic, and it is with that that I wish to begin. I was born into a country and into a family with strong Christian traditions. I call that basic, although it is neither a necessary nor a sufficient condition of being a Christian. It is clearly not a necessary condition, for there are many convinced Christians today who were born into situations governed by long-standing traditions of opposition to Christianity. It is equally clearly not a sufficient condition, for there are also many, born into the same kind of tradition that I was, who firmly repudiate any allegiance to the Christian faith. Nonetheless, it still seems to me that the situation of my birth is one important factor in my being a Christian today. The point that I am trying to make is sometimes put in the form: 'If I had been born in Sri Lanka or in Thailand, I would probably be a Buddhist.' If by that statement we mean simply that statistically there are more Buddhists than Christians in Sri Lanka or in Thailand and more Christians than Buddhists in this country, that of course is true. And it follows that in any random sample of Sri Lankans or Thais one is likely to find more Buddhists than Christians, whereas in any random sample of the inhabitants of this country one is likely to find the reverse. But the point was not made in that coldly statistical form. The way in which I

I

made it, which is the way in which it is often made in such a context as this, was: 'If I had been born in Sri Lanka or in Thailand, I would probably be a Buddhist.' But that seems to me a misleading way of putting it – and significantly misleading because it derives some of its force from the misleading way in which it is put. For who is this 'I' who might equally well have been a Sri Lankan or a Thai? Is it some bare substratum of a human self, which could equally well be fitted out with any set of human characteristics? Is the real 'I' a number on the heavenly computer, so that if some Sri Lankan mother had given birth (or conceived) one second before rather than one second after my mother did, that would have been the slot that I would have occupied as in strict rotation I was rolled off the divine conveyor-belt? No, the only 'I' which has any meaning for me is an 'I' with the specific genetic and environmental heritage into which I was born. However much later circumstance and conscious decision may alter my attitude to Christianity, my initial relation to it remains. I absorbed something of its ethos with my mother's milk. There I was put; I could do no other.

This fundamental contingency of our human existence is something we all recognize. Each of us is who he or she is and not another one. But how important is that fact to the beliefs and practices of our later life? We are used to the idea of people following in their parents' footsteps. If the child of gifted mathematicians turns out himself to be a mathematician, we do not regard that as a matter of pure chance; but nor do we consider it relevant to an evaluation of his mathematical discoveries. An artist born and brought up within one particular artistic tradition may find it difficult to appreciate differing traditions at the same level of appreciation. The images, the style, the fundamental conception of what great art is, with which he was brought up, may so have affected his basic awareness that he cannot wholly free himself from them in his response to art of any kind.

Where does the religious person stand? There are no clear-cut tests for the truth of his or her beliefs of a kind that the mathematician and, up to a point, the natural scientist can apply. He is more like the artist, for value-judgments and deep-seated imagery are a part alike of the content of his beliefs and the criteria by which he has to assess them. That is not to say that he is inescapably trapped within the tradition of his birth and upbringing. Those are, as we have seen, neither necessary nor sufficient conditions of religious belief. There is such a thing as conversion. People move in and out of faith, and can (sometimes, at least) give coherent reasons for doing so. But they are the exception rather than the rule. To be born within a religious tradition greatly increases the probability of a person's coming to believe and adhere to that religion for himself. We all know that to be true as a matter of statistics. What I have been seeking to convey is something more than statistical probability, a sense of how deeply that fact is embedded within religious faith itself. For whatever part philosophical argument and historical evidence may play, religious faith is never a matter of logical deduction from such reasoning. It is a response of the whole person to the totality of the environment in which he finds himself. And a fundamental part, both of his being as a person and of the environment in which he finds himself, is the religious tradition (if any) into which he is born.

So my being born into a Christian tradition is not the sole reason for my being a Christian today. But it seems to me now a far more important factor than I would have allowed it to be thirty years ago. Moreover, it is not just an external fact about my faith to be acknowledged and then set on one side in further reflection about and practice of that faith. For the reasons that I have tried to outline, it is something that must be allowed to enter into and to affect my understanding of that faith and the way in which I hold it. Many Christians are reluctant to take that further step – and for understandable reasons. Does it not inevitably involve a weakening of the conviction that our faith is grounded objectively in the truth? And does it not therefore involve a weakening of our commitment to that faith in practice?

John Taylor has made this point forcefully in a lecture on 'The Theological Basis of Interfaith Dialogue'.[1] Writing as a Christian, but one with a profound and appreciative knowledge of other faiths, he speaks of something 'which is in fact common to us all . . . what I would call the "jealousies" of the different faiths. I mean those points in every religion concerning which the believers are inwardly compelled to claim a universal significance and finality.' He goes on to 'plead with those who want to make all the intractable convictions relative and level them down for the sake of a quick reconciliation: leave us at least our capacity for categorical assertion, for that is what we have in common.' He is surely right to insist on the absoluteness of conviction which is an integral feature not only of Christian but also of other religious faiths. But once we recognize this absoluteness of conviction as characteristic of differing religious faiths, something demanding to be treated with respect in each case, we cannot be content that our capacity for categorical assertion be left wholly unchallenged. To do so would be to rule out not only quick reconciliation but long-term reconciliation also. Moreover, it would not be to treat the other person's categorical assertion with true seriousness or genuine respect.

The position in which we find ourselves is one which seems to call at the same time for an absoluteness of commitment and a recognition of the limitation of our own perspective, both as individuals and as the Christian community. Do without the first and there is a crippling loss of religious vitality; do without the second and there is a danger not merely of absolutizing our own perspective but of religious fanaticism as well. But if the combination is desirable, is it in fact possible? The tension is real enough. It may never wholly disappear. Neither pole must be abandoned. But if we are willing to allow the form alike of the absoluteness and of the limitation to be the subject of critical scrutiny, it is possible that both can be apprehended as positive components in a coherent form of religious faith. To ask how this can be done pushes us back to reconsider the grounds of our believing at all and the character of the language by which we give expression to that belief.

Religion, like language itself, is to be found not in one universal form, but in a multiplicity of diverse forms. Artificial attempts to create a single religious esperanto are as lifeless as in the linguistic case. It may be that there is some deep structure, some universal grammar of religion, but if so it is as inaccessible to us as its equivalent in language. What we have to do with are particular religions with their specific imageries and traditions. But they speak to us, and intend to speak to us, of that which is universal. The universal referent is grasped, and can only be grasped, in and through the particular form. And the particular form is only grasped in a genuinely religious way when it speaks to us of that which is universal. Yet the universality and the absoluteness which characterize that to which it refers are not characteristics inherent in the form itself. To treat the form as if they were, to give to it the absoluteness that belongs rightly to its referent, is the sin of idolatry. So as a Christian, entered into a particular tradition of religious faith, I have no choice but to be critically reflective about the form of faith to which I adhere. Such critical reflection is not negative in itself, though of course the way in which it is conducted and the outcome to which it leads may be so in particular cases. But the activity can be an essential part of the way of faith itself, at least of any faith in the prophetic tradition which insists on the distinction between holy objects in the life of faith and the ultimate reality which they mediate. It can contribute to that process by which we internalize and make our own the tradition of our faith.

But before embarking on that process I must first take the full measure of the contingency of my standpoint in faith. For there is not only a geographical but also a historical contingency about it. I was born not only in a particular place but at a particular time. What I have said about the likely difference had 'I' been born into a Buddhist family in Thailand could be said also about 'my' being born into a Christian family four hundred or more years earlier. For religions differ not only from other religions at the same time; despite that conservative tendency which is a general characteristic of religion, they differ also from earlier manifestations of themselves.

The fact of such change is not in doubt. To describe its true character is a much more difficult task. We can point to the emergence of new beliefs and of new dogmas. It is not so easy to determine where they represent the formal codification of convictions that have long been implicit in the faith and practice of earlier Christians, and where they represent genuine novelty. But that there are some instances of real changes in belief seems to me beyond dispute. It is also possible to claim that sometimes where the formulas have remained unaltered their meaning has significantly changed.[2] Thus 'no salvation outside the church' meant something very different to Cyprian from what it meant to Jacques Maritain, who reinterprets it in terms of 'the soul of the church' and understands it to mean that 'there is no salvation outside the truth' or 'for those who sin against the light'.[3] What are of greatest interest and of greatest difficulty to trace are what I would call changes in the basic apprehension of Christian faith, in the root sense of what it is to be a Christian believer. Of course there is a measure of continuity down the ages, but I am convinced that there have also been important changes at the level of fundamental feeling.[4] One of the best attempts to chart this difficult terrain is Keith Thomas' survey of popular beliefs in sixteenth- and seventeenth-century England. At the end of his long and extensively illustrated account, he is led to conclude that it

> was not simply a matter of religion driving out its rivals, for the religion which survived the decline of magic was not the

religion of Tudor England. When the Devil was banished to Hell, God himself was confined to working through natural causes. 'Special providences' and private revelations gave way to the notion of a Providence which itself obeyed natural laws accessible to human study . . . So although our period ended with the triumph of religion, it was religion with a difference.[5]

In his frequently reprinted *Practice of Piety*, first written early in the seventeenth century, Lewis Bayly attributes repeated fires at Stratford-on-Avon and at Tiverton to God's judgment on the profaning of the Sabbath in those two towns. In his diary, Ralph Josselin interpreted the death of his ten-day-old son from diptheria on 23 February 1648 as (in part at least) a punishment imposed on him by God for his excessive fondness of chess.[6] The religion of such men would indeed seem to be 'religion with a difference' from that which I and, I suspect, all my fellow clergy in the Church of England today profess. Yet Bayly was Bishop of Bangor for fifteen years and Ralph Josselin was Vicar of Earls Colne for forty-two. Their religion was the religion of Anglican clergy every bit as much as ours, only they lived three centuries earlier. And the difference is not minor or peripheral; it concerns the basic character of God and the way in which he directs and affects our daily life. Indeed, we do not have to look further than the Book of Common Prayer to see the fundamental character of the changes involved. Geoffrey Lampe draws attention to its prayers 'for times of pestilence (plague being deliberately sent by God in the execution of his justice, and the escape of any survivors being due to his undeserved mercy), and for the visitation of the sick (who should regard illness either as a punishment for sin in the case of the wicked or as a trial of faith for the righteous)', and concludes in a phrase closely reminiscent of Keith Thomas' language: 'Such changes are so profound as to transform Christianity from time to time into almost a different religion from what it was before.'[7]

It is easy enough to say that the particular form of the belief of those earlier generations of Christians was influenced by the attitudes and knowledge of their time. No doubt it was. But so equally undoubtedly is mine. So as I reflect upon those beliefs, my recognition of the changing pattern of Christian belief down the ages forces me from another angle to recognize that, however perfect and however permanent may be that reality of which my beliefs speak, the beliefs themselves cannot partake either of perfection or of permanence.

But the faith that I hold, I hold not simply as a Christian who is conscious that there are other religious traditions of profound spirituality, nor simply as a twentieth-century Christian who is conscious of the ambiguous relation between the forms of Christian faith practised today and those of earlier generations. I hold it also as member of a society in which many people of great integrity, intelligence and sensitivity repudiate religious belief of any kind. I cannot dismiss their convictions as patently absurd, morally or intellectually. If I am to hold my own faith with integrity, the scope of my critical reflection upon that faith must extend beyond the particularities of its form to which our earlier considerations have led us. It must concern itself also with the yet more fundamental question: is the basic religious conviction itself mistaken? Is it true that there is an absolute or universal referent of any kind towards which the varied forms of religion point? Since the absolute, or universal, if accessible to us at all, is only accessible through some specific form or object, these two types of reflection cannot be wholly separated from one another. But a measure of distinction between them can be usefully maintained.

What form, then, is appropriate to critical reflection about the basic validity of religious belief? It is important to stress at the outset that what we are engaged in here is a reflection upon something that exists. We are not setting out to see if it is possible for people to hold religious beliefs of this ultimate kind. They already do. What we are trying to do is to consider whether those beliefs are a delusion or whether there is some ultimate referent to which they point, some ultimate reality on which all else depends.

Such reflection is a more prominent feature of theology today than it was a few decades ago. Many theologians at that time regarded it as of little or no importance, because they held 'the belief of dialectical theology that it is possible to accept atheist arguments and trump them by a radical belief in revelation'. But that conviction has been justly described by Pannenberg as guilty of the very fault of which it accused others, namely of being 'an excessive adaptation of theology to the intellectual fashions of the age'.[8] So reflection of the kind of which we are now speaking is more generally recognized today as being an inescapable necessity.

But how can such reflection be carried out? Can it be more than the religious believer acting as judge about the validity of his own belief and declaring it valid? It cannot wholly escape that kind of difficulty, for it is one which inevitably besets any critical review of fundamental presuppositions or convictions, religious or otherwise. But that does not mean that it is a mere facade, that the element of critical reflection is no more than a form of self-deception. The kind of reasoning to which appeal is made has close parallels in other areas of human experience.[9] Moreover, the reflection involved draws on a far wider range of human experience than just the explicitly religious. To quote Pannenberg again, 'the conflict between theology and atheism, the decision about whether any way can be found to the idea of God depends on the understanding of man, upon anthropology'.[10] Even that statement may be said to draw the net more narrowly than it should be drawn. Indeed Pannenberg himself goes on in the next sentence to insist on the importance of our understanding of the world also in this context. But it is on the anthropological aspect, to which he gives pride of place, that I wish to concentrate here.[11] Such an approach seeks to show that the reference to an ultimate, which is the nub of religious believing, also characterizes in a more hidden way all the most fundamental forms of human experience. Different theologians have pursued this line of enquiry in varying ways. They vary both in terms of the aspect of human experience that they analyse and in terms of the philosophical method and terminology they use. But despite important differences, there is a more important similarity of approach to be noted here in the work of many theologians whose methods are in other respects remarkably diverse.

In his article on 'Anthropology and the Question of God', Pannenberg refers to the work of Brunner and Tillich, of Rahner, Nygren and Ebeling, of Max Scheler and John Cobb.[12] Though critical of most of them, he sees their work as pointing in the right direction. The list could easily be extended. What is characteristic of this approach is its depiction of the most fundamental aspects of our experience as apparently postulating that absolute, unconditioned reality of which religion speaks. We recognize, for example, that our own individual knowing, and that of every other individual human being – in other words, of every knowing subject of which we know – is limited and relative, each to its own particular perspective. Yet the very recognition of that all-pervading relativity involves the fleeting grasp of something beyond relativity, of an objectivity that we envisage but cannot attain.[13] Men like Sartre or Camus insist on the absurdity, the utter meaninglessness of life. Yet by the vigour of their moral protest against such meaninglessness, they appear to have stepped beyond it and inadvertently suggested that meaninglessness does not have the last word.[14] These kinds of consideration apply not merely to the more personal or existential aspects of our experience. They apply to all human experience, including not least our modern scientific knowledge. Thus Hans Küng speaks of a fundamental trust in reality as the basis of both science and ethics, and sees that same fundamental trust as pointing towards (though not simply to be identified with) religious faith.[15] The universality of operation of such an attitude is summed up by Schubert Ogden when he confesses that he 'can only conclude that faith in God as the ground of confidence in life's ultimate meaning is the necessary condition of our existence as selves'.[16]

If there is force in this approach, we must be careful not to claim too much for it. Ogden speaks of it as 'the only really essential "proof of God's existence" '.[17] His inverted commas suggest that the words within them are being used in a somewhat Pickwickian sense. For it is something less than 'proof' that is involved here. Pannenberg, who as we have seen is no less insistent on the absolute necessity of such an approach, is less assertive about the measure of its achievement. For he allows it 'as possible that man's very nature is dependent upon an illusion which, contrary to what is held by atheist theories of illusion, he is not able to detect as such, because it is in the nature of his being always to be subject to it'. And in view of that he argues that 'general anthropological considerations can never take us further than the assertion that when man's being is fully aware, man is conscious that he is dependent upon a reality which surpasses and sustains everything finite, and in this sense is a divine reality'.[18] Moreover, as those words imply, it is not only the probative force of the approach that must be qualified, but the sense in which that to which it points may be called 'God'. For if that word is to be used, we must be careful to remember, as Pannenberg insists elsewhere, that whatever the argument may be thought to have established, it must not be regarded as having established the validity of the full Christian understanding of God.[19]

But that is not to deny its significance. Our starting-point was the experience of being a religious believer within a society where it is very difficult to deny the problematic character of religious belief as such. In moments of worship or of Christian fellowship, our belief may seem wholly self-authenticating. But we cannot deny the possibility that we may be deluded. Does religious belief survive the scrutiny of a more detached reflection in a cool hour? Or will it disappear in the harsh light of a critical analysis? In general, such critical analysis changes the situation less markedly than might have been expected. It does not do away with the problematic character of faith. It neither shows religious belief to be something demonstrably unreasonable, nor does it 'prove' the reality of the divine. It shows that the basic religious conviction is not automatically dissolved by the acids of criticism and that there is a comparably problematic character about the position of those who deny any form of ultimate or divine reality. Moreover, it shows that this basic religious conviction is not just an extra belief that some people may happen to have alongside and in addition to their other beliefs. It can be seen more clearly for what the religious person always believed it to be, something that underlies all human existence. So we may claim for this kind of reflection two things. First, that it enables us to continue in the path of religious conviction and practice with greater confidence that we are not acting in bad faith, that we are not simply continuing in an attractive tradition that has to be kept at arm's length from critical examination. But more than that, it opens the way to a deeper awareness of the all-pervasive nature of the divine, of its fundamental bearing upon the whole range of human experience. And that is an insight that must not be forgotten or overlooked as we affirm and practise the particular religious beliefs of our own tradition.

In what I have said so far, I have spoken mainly of 'that which is ultimate' or of 'the divine'. I have used the word 'God' sparingly to avoid any implication that reflections of the kind I have been pursuing point us directly to God as known in Christian faith. For the God to whom I commit myself as a Christian is a personal God, the living God, a God of love. The two conceptions are not identical, but there is no necessary conflict between the impersonal language to which I have so far restricted myself and the more personal language of Christian theism. For if 'the ultimate' or 'the divine' is that in which our experience of knowing and of acting, our very existence as human selves, is grounded, it cannot be wholly alien in character from what it is to be a person. There may be grave difficulties in making sense of some of the more directly personal ways in which Christians speak of God. Indeed, almost the whole history of Christian theology could be presented as a continuing struggle with just that issue. We have seen already how easily talk of God's personal action in the world can take forms that are wholly unacceptable to us. And while it is in statements from past ages that the difficulties tend to impinge most forcefully on us, we ought to acknowledge that our own ways of speaking of God's personal action may be open to similar objections. But we have no cause to fear that the personal language itself is altogether out of place. If our sense of ultimacy is rightly grounded in anthropological reflection of the kind I have indicated, the use of personal terms and personal concepts in relation to God cannot be wholly inappropriate. But if this personal language about God is to be the language of my personal faith and not the vestigial remains of an ancient piety to which I simply continue to conform, I must probe more fully how it is to be understood. It is a central feature of the Christian tradition in which I stand, and I must try to enter into it also by the process of critical reflection.

Our rejection of Lewis Bayly's explanation of the town fires which were so frequent a feature of life in the seventeenth century and of Ralph Josselin's interpretation of his son's death was based primarily on moral grounds. The idea that they were actions of the personal and living God and that their reason was punishment for profaning the sabbath in the one case and for Josselin's love of chess on the other is utterly abhorrent to our moral consciousness. But moral grounds of that kind leave it open to us to interpret the recovery of a child from illness in comparable circumstances as God's personal act. Even if, as Thomas suggests, we may be led to confine God's way of working to natural causes, that does not prevent us from seeing such a recovery as God's action. But two doubts hold me back from claiming that a modification of this kind, a changed assessment of what actions and what motives should be ascribed to God, is all that needs to be done.

If the propitious happening is ascribed to the action of God, while the otherwise similar but unpropitious happening is not, is there not something arbitrary and unconvincing about such discrimination? If I believed in the devil, a supernatural power of evil at war with God on the battleground of the world, such a divided ascription of the ultimate agency of what happens might make sense. But that is not a belief I find it possible to hold. Moreover, if God can and does act in the sort of way that we are here considering, there is another form of arbitrariness that seems to be involved, an arbitrariness not simply in our discrimination but in the activity of God himself. For not to act where one could act is itself a form of 'action'. If we ascribe the fortunate eventualities of life to God's action in this way, do we not thereby increase the difficulty of seeing the world as in the hands of a moral and loving God to the level of an impossibility?

Let me illustrate this familiar problem with two examples, both from the period of the Second World War. In 1940 a far greater proportion of the British Expeditionary Force succeeded in getting away from the Dunkirk beaches than had at one time looked likely thanks in no small measure to a spell of exceptionally fine weather. Many people at the time attributed that fine weather to the intervention of God. But if such is a conceivable form of God's action in the world, we cannot but wonder at God's apparent inaction in other comparable cases of human need. My other example is the story of the son of a Presbyterian minister recounted by Sydney Evans, and I tell it in his words:

On three occasions, shortly after being posted from one destroyer to another, the destroyer he had left was sunk. The old father interpreted this as evidence of special providential care. His son rejected this interpretation as he saw no reason why he should have been singled out for special treatment when his former companions died.[20]

Reflections such as these lead me to stress the need for extreme caution in laying claim to any knowledge of just where or how God's action is to be seen in what happens in the world. Sydney Evans goes on to speak of a 'direction in events', 'a kind of moral grain in the Universe'.[21] I myself followed a similar line of approach in *The Remaking of Christian Doctrine*.[22] But I felt bound to describe it there as having, in one sense of the word, a 'deistic' character about it. Certainly it can be claimed with justice that such a conception is closely related to the broader theme of an overall divine purpose for the world, which is an important aspect of biblical and later Christian thought. But can we escape the feeling that in some important way it falls short of the living and personal God, with whom the biblical tradition and the continuing faith of the church is concerned? Faith seeks to speak of God as living and active in relation to the actualities of life. Is that a mistaken desire? Or does it at least have to be demythologized into some much more generalized and theoretical statement about God as creator of a world capable of expressing his purposes for good and as the primary cause of all being and of all acting? Such ideas are important, religiously as well as philosophically. But something more personal and more direct seems also to be called for by the religious consciousness. How can that something more be understood?

2

The Language of Faith: Creation and Disclosure

In the process of critical reflection about Christian faith on which I have embarked, I have so far found less difficulty in reassuring myself about the existence of some transcendent referent of experience, some reality corresponding to the word 'God', than in reassuring myself about God's personal, active involvement in the world. Yet the latter is vital to Christian faith. Without it, belief in God would be a philosophical idea of general interest, but hardly a passionate conviction of fundamental personal significance. Am I then faced with an insoluble conflict between the postulates of faith and the reasoned judgment of theological reflection? As I have already insisted, I certainly cannot rest content with any absolute disjunction between the two. Theological reflection is parasitic upon the life of faith and cannot survive a sundering of the links between them. In that respect the old tag, *lex orandi lex credendi*, is a valid principle. The reflective formulations of faith must be consistent with the experienced actuality of faith. But we are in danger of misconstruing the very real problem with which this *prima facie* conflict between faith and theological reflection presents us, if we overlook the important differences of style and language between the two. *Lex orandi lex credendi* may be a sound principle, but *vox orandi vox credendi* is not. The use of language in the articulation of faith in prayer and worship is very different from the use of

17

language in critical reflection.

If we are to answer the question with which the last chapter ended, we need to clarify these uses of language and the differences between them. What, then, is the distinctive character of the language of faith? In its Preface, the *Good News Bible* declares its intention 'to use language that is natural, clear, simple and unambiguous'. That sounds a wholly praiseworthy aim. It would seem on first hearing to be a valuable reminder that the Bible is a primary document of faith and not a secondary work of theological scholarship, and that the language used in any translation of it must do justice to that fact. Yet it has come in for some trenchant criticism. Stephen Prickett declares any such aim to be an impossibility 'because religion is *not about* things that are natural, clear, simple and unambiguous'.[1] Prickett was certainly not asking that the language should be forced, obscure, complex and equivocating. Indeed he goes on to claim the unqualified support of generations of poets, sages, saints and divines. It is simplicity of a different kind that is being called for. Mathematical concepts, like odd and even, can be clear and simple because they are purely abstract. Personal terms, like love and hate, are not obscure and complicated; but nor are they clear and simple in the same way that mathematical concepts are. They are opposites, like odd and even. But we know from experience that they do not exclude one another in the absolute way that odd and even do. And the way we use them in language needs to reflect this complexity or ambiguity of our experience.

Problems of this kind are even more acute in the case of religious language, as we seek to speak about that which is ultimate. So how does such language function? It takes hold of certain images that are basic to our experience of life and extends their meaning so that they point to what is ultimate. Where such images establish themselves as effective pointers for that purpose, they become symbols of that which cannot be directly spoken.[2] So religious language may appropriately be described as a form of 'imaginative construction' or of 'symbol-ization'.[3]

Such a description of religious language is likely to raise hackles of suspicion in many minds. It appears to threaten the objectivity of the language, to undermine religion's concern with reality. For does it not assimilate the language of religion to that of literature or poetry, and is not that to view it in a more subjective light than the person of faith either is or should be prepared to allow? The analogy with literature or poetry is certainly there. It is the implication so frequently drawn from that analogy that must be resisted.[4]

To stress the imaginative character of poetic and of religious language is not to suggest that their concern is with the purely imaginary. The language of poetry is often more ambiguous than that of mathematics and more indirect than that of every-day speech; but it is emphatically not imprecise. The imagina-tion indeed has recently been defined as 'the intellect in quest of appropriate precision'.[5] No one is more concerned about the 'rightness' of a particular word in a particular context than the poet. The poet's criteria of precision will be no less exacting than those with which the mathematician works, though they will be different.[6] But the difference between them is not to be thought of as one between correspondence with fact on the one hand and some purely subjective standard of artistic propriety on the other. 'In the sense in which it gives us an insight into the nature of things', writes Mary Warnock, 'the imagination is the source not merely of passing pleasures or *frissons* . . . but of *truth.*'[7] The poet is concerned to depict what is real in a way which no other form of language is able to communicate. Indeed, he may claim not merely to depict but even to create reality. Such a power can be ascribed to something as apparently simple as the use of metaphor itself. Thus Paul Ricoeur writes:

A discourse which makes use of metaphor has the extra-ordinary power of redescribing reality. . . . metaphor not only shatters the previous structures of our language, but also the previous structures of what we call reality. When we ask whether metaphorical language reaches reality, we presuppose that we already know what reality is. But if we assume that metaphor redescribes reality, we must then assume that this reality as redescribed is itself novel reality. With metaphor we experience the metamorphosis of both language and reality.[8]

And Max Black advocates a 'strong creativity thesis with regard to metaphor, according to which metaphors sometimes function as ' "cognitive instruments", indispensable for perceiving connections that, once perceived, are *then* truly present'.[9] If such strong claims can be made for metaphorical discourse in general, it should come as little surprise to find poetry described by Jacques Maritain as a 'recomposition of a world more real than the reality offered to the senses',[10] and poetic language spoken of by Philip Wheelwright as 'partly creating and partly disclosing certain hitherto unknown, unguessed at aspects of What Is'.[11] Descriptions of the artistic imagination as involving both creation and disclosure are not uncommon. Eliseo Vivas has entitled a collection of his essays in criticism and aesthetics *Creation and Discovery*. 'Art,' he writes in the preface, 'both *creates* and *discovers* values and meanings.'[12] And in one of the essays, he goes on to compare the work of the poet to the creative work of God as described in Gen. 1.2:

> Before the poet comes along, the earth, for us, is without form and void, and darkness is upon the face of the deep. The poet divides the light from the darkness, and gives us an ordered world.[13]

So, too, Max Black describes the conception of metaphor presented in the essay from which we have already quoted as 'grounded in analogies of structure (partly created, partly discovered).'[14] If such descriptions of metaphor and poetry are valid, there is no need to fear that an approach to religious language by way of comparison with the poetic will automatically commit us to an unacceptably subjective view of religious faith.

But even if we have succeeded in exorcising the fear that the approach being proposed is bound to lead to unduly subjective or reductionist conclusions, we have still to ask how it is to be applied in the sphere of religious faith. If someone speaks of life as a journey, we are tempted to say that that is mere metaphor; that life remains life, however we choose to describe it. But if someone seriously sees his or her life as a journey, with its implication of choosing a route towards some goal, this cannot fail to make the life he experiences a fundamentally different reality from what it would have been had he been equally seriously convinced that life was an illusion. The language of his faith is an imaginative construction. But that is not to say that it is purely subjective or imaginary; it does not involve regarding it as non-cognitive in character.[15] What the language of faith does for the believer is to disclose something that was always a potential in God's world and make it a reality for him. It doesn't merely redescribe his life; or rather in redescribing it, it makes it into something different – a journey of the human spirit on the path towards God. In Wheelwright's phrase, it is something that both discloses and is creative of reality.[16]

The application to the language of faith of Wheelwright's description of poetic language as providing disclosures of reality has a familiar ring. It was a phrase much used in the writings of Ian Ramsey. Moreover, it clearly affirms the cognitive character of such language. But to speak of the language of faith as *creating* reality sounds strange, if not inconsistent with the essentially responsive and receptive character of faith itself. But I believe that if it is treated as supplementary to the idea of disclosing reality, it is both justified and illuminating. Seeing life as a journey is, I have argued, one example of the creative power of a simple metaphor within a religious context. Peter Slater has argued the case for this dual function of symbolic or analogical language with just this sort of case in mind.

> The implication of the term 'disclosure' is that there is something previously there to be disclosed. And this, of course, is one reason why Christian apologists like the term. But a non-reductive account of metaphors and models gives them a more dynamic role than this in structuring the realities of meaningful life. This is especially true of symbols which serve in making decisions concerning roles and goals rather than disclosures concerning matters of fact. The element of creativity in our use of symbols makes our situation more open to novelty and change than traditional doctrines of analogy and talk of disclosure have allowed.[17]

But it is important that the disclosive and creative functions of religious language should not be regarded as incompatible alternatives. The choice of roles and goals is a free and creative choice; but that is not to say that it is wholly unfettered, or that there are no limits to the range of creative possibilities open to us. Life is not straightforwardly a journey; nor is that the only valid way of seeing life. But seeing life that way is a valid choice, because it corresponds in some measure to the transcendent reality of our existence. It is at the same time creative of the particular reality by which we live, and also a part of the process by which we receive some insight and disclosure into the already existing structures of the world.

Before we move on to our primary task of applying this understanding of the dual nature of the language of faith to some of the central issues in Christian theology, it is worth noting that it is of far-reaching significance for a problem which we encountered at an earlier stage. It enables us to understand better the situation of apparent conflict between different faiths, each of which appears to have a good claim to be a genuine form of religious apprehension.[18] The recognition that religious language 'partly creates What Is' enables us to do justice to the real differences between such faiths; for it is a reminder how the particular languages of the differing traditions have contributed to the creation of different realities. Yet the parallel insistence that religious language also 'partly discloses What Is' enables us to do justice to the conviction that, even in and through those differences, both have to do with the same fundamental reality. And it is a framework of that kind that any constructive dialogue of religions requires. For we need to be able to acknowledge with equal conviction the unity of the ultimate religious reality with which both are engaged and the diversity of our particular apprehensions of it. H. R. Schlette speaks of how 'human beings with religious affiliations are becoming conscious of their common though differently patterned life in the presence of the transcendent mystery'.[19] What the approach with which we are working has to offer is a more precise understanding both of what it is that is common and of how the different patternings arise.

It is not only in an inter-religious context that a proper recognition of the imaginative or symbolic character of religious language can save us from dangerous forms of misunderstanding. 'Faith,' says Tillich, 'if it takes its symbols literally becomes idolatrous.'[20] But even if that negative point be granted readily enough, something more still needs to be said if we are to justify the positive conviction that, taken symbolically, the language of our faith is capable of disclosing and creating something which we apprehend as reality, that it is something more, to use Brian Gerrish's language, than 'the free play of the artistic imagination'.[21] Religious language is always poised on a knife-edge between affirming nonsense and lapsing into vacuity – which is not to say that it is bound to end up doing one or the other. But the risk is always there, on the one hand of treating our religious affirmations about, for example, acts of God, so simplistically that they are patently false, or on the other of giving them so sophisticated a meaning that it makes no difference whether we say that God acts or that he does not act. If stress on the symbolic character of the language preserves us from the first fate, we need still to confirm the power of those symbols to disclose reality if we are to be sure that we have not succumbed to the second.

Let us, therefore, look more closely at one of the basic images or symbols of Christian faith in its traditional speech about God's relation to the world. Christians speak of God as 'Father'. That's simple enough, but it's not clear or unambiguous. Christians use it of God as creator of the universe; they use it of his relation to the whole human race made in his image, of his particular relation to Christian believers made his sons and daughters by adoption and grace, and more specifically still of his special relation to Jesus.[22] In no case does the word 'Father' directly describe what that relation is. But it has found acceptance because it is felt to disclose some reality already there, already dimly sensed. And in redescribing that reality in terms of 'Father', it also brings into being a novel reality. And it does so in this way. Our relation to God is something much bigger, much more pervasive than our awareness of it. But we are meant to be aware of it. It cannot come to its intended fruition without our becoming conscious of it. And that needs words. So when the image of God as Father came to be used and the symbol of God's fatherhood had been established, something new was brought into existence. What had been only potential in God's world – namely human life as consciously determined by the sense of God as Father – had become actual. The language had partly disclosed but thereby had also partly created previously unknown and unguessed at aspects of What Is.

But where the symbol unites, theological reflection discriminates. It seeks to check and to control the play of the shafts of light that come from the one symbol. It lays down distinctions between the way in which God's fatherhood is to be understood in the various contexts. But it is liable to overplay its hand. It speaks at times as if the various relationships that the theologian is seeking to distinguish could be expressed in non-symbolic language that would make the symbol itself dispensable. But that is to overlook the secondary status of theological reflection. When theology exceeds the bounds of its proper function in that way, it can justly be criticized as 'a blasphemous form of anti-poetry'.[23] But that charge cannot be properly directed, as Tennant sought to direct it, against theology as such. For theology has an important role to play in relation to the faith which gives rise to it. That role is not to replace the language of symbol with non-symbolic statements, any more than it is the task of the literary critic to render the poem about which he writes dispensable. Sometimes, it is true, the literary critic may show that the imagery of a poem is weak, and its symbols dead, that it gives rise to no clear or creative vision. The result of his work may then be that the reading public, and perhaps the poet himself also, will be content to allow the poem to pass into oblivion. Others in course of time will take its place. So, too, the theologian may show that some religious symbols are dead or have become misleading.[24] 'Sacrifice' loses its force as an image when literal sacrifices are no longer a popular feature of religious practice; 'king' is liable to change its symbolic significance as the role of the king undergoes radical change in human society. No symbol indeed is altogether immune from such change, as contemporary difficulties arising from the exclusively male character of the term 'father' illustrate. The language of faith cannot be completely unchanging. But it is more flexible and more resilient than the conceptual language of theology. More often, what the work both of the literary critic and of the theologian does is to disclose new depths of meaning in poem or in religious symbol that have not been grasped before. His ideal is to send the reader or the person of faith back to his poem or to the practice of his faith, enabling them to find in their symbols a more profound meaning.

But Christian faith is not just a system of images and symbols designed to evoke an apprehension of God in relation to the

world here and now. It speaks of a continuing historical purpose in terms of which we are to understand the meaning of our
lives. And it describes that historical purpose not in ordinary
historical terms but as a series of divine acts. 'Act of God' is not
so obviously metaphorical a phrase as 'fatherhood of God', and
some theologians have insisted that the word 'act' is to be
understood in a non-symbolical or univocal sense.[25] But Tillich
is surely right when he warns against such understanding of the
language. 'A second level of primary religious symbolism,' he
wrote, 'is the way in which religion speaks of divine actions like
creation, providence, miracles, incarnation, consummation etc.
It is especially important to emphasize the symbolic character
of these symbols, because they often are understood literally . . .
[with the result that] the whole relation of God and the world
becomes a nest of absurdities.'[26]

If we accept the language of God acting as symbolic, we find
that, just as in the case of the fatherhood of God, the Bible
brings together many diverse types of happening under this one
image: the creation of the world, the establishment of Israel as
a nation with the aid of such miraculous occurrences as the
crossing of the Red Sea and the fall of Jericho, the return from
exile as a result of the military exploits of the heathen king
Cyrus, and the life of Jesus with its contrasts of apparently
God-forsaken crucifixion and miraculous resurrection. All these
the person of faith holds together under the illuminating and
uniting symbol of the purposive activity of God, and weaves
them together into a single story. Here again the theologian
discriminates, and seeks to distinguish different senses in which
the one symbol can be held to refer to so many very diverse
types of happening. But here too he must resist the temptation
to think of his task as one of replacing the symbolic story with a
more direct, non-symbolic account. His task is rather to reflect
on the uses of the symbol of divine action in the traditions of
Christian faith and on our general understanding of how things
happen in the world, in such a way that the symbol may disclose

to us a new reality, transcending but not simply standing in conflict with our ordinary understanding of the world. This was the problem with which we were faced at the end of the last chapter and which prompted our investigation into the nature of religious language. Does it in fact suggest ways in which that problem can be overcome?

The heart of the problem is the natural tendency to understand divine action in terms of efficient causation. It is understanding divine action in that sense that leads most directly to the impasse in which we found ourselves. But it is questionable how far that way of understanding it is compatible with a symbolic interpretation of the language. When we speak of God as the father of Christian believers we are using a symbol which partly discloses an existing reality of our dependence on the creative love of God and partly creates a new reality by bringing that existing reality to consciousness in a distinctively new way. Can some similar interpretation be given of those 'providential' occurrences which we describe as God's acts of mercy and judgment?

In the first place, 'act of God' is a symbol which discloses an existing reality, namely that there are occurrences in the world which embody and express (in substantial if not in perfect measure) the will of God, either for mankind in general or for a particular person. But such symbols, we have been claiming, do not only disclose reality; they also create it. By symbolizing certain occurrences as God's acts, we create a new reality. Just as by means of the symbol of divine fatherhood the world is recognized and experienced as depending on a source other and greater than itself, whose fundamental character towards it is one of love, so by the symbol of divine action certain occurrences within the world are acknowledged and experienced as having a special and intimate relation to that ultimate source of love. In the past that special relation has normally been understood in terms of efficient causation. God has been seen either as replacing some missing link in the causal chain that would normally have been expected, or as some higher order of causal agent controlling the particular causal chain as a whole. The first description corresponds to events described as miraculous, the latter to events with no overtly miraculous features but which are regarded as providentially guided. Neither account can be formally disproved, since causal chains at the purely human level of explanation are never complete or exhaustive in themselves. Nevertheless, they do seem to have become not merely implausible and superfluous from the standpoint of human explanation, but religiously unsatisfactory in view of their apparently occasional and highly selective character. But is it possible to conceive this special and intimate relation of certain events to the ultimate source of divine love in some other way or has the symbol of divine action become empty of genuine content? What is this new reality that the symbol not only discloses but creates?

Let us begin with a human analogy. The life of a people may be rigidly circumscribed over long periods of time by a subsistence economy and an unchanging social order. That experience provides them with defining and confining criteria of the real and the possible. But no patterns of experience are totally uniform or unchanging. And if some aspects of that static order of existence are grasped as embodying, however imperfectly, a measure of change, then a new reality is born. New possibilities for people's lives begin to be imagined; new visions of the future arise; powerful forces for further and much greater measures of change emerge. So at the religious level: the imaginative construction, whereby certain occurrences in human history are seen symbolically as God's acts, gives rise to an experience of the world as a place where God's will can be, in some measure at least, both grasped and realized. Such a change is not simply a new description of the old reality; it is the emergence of a new reality. For the events which are seen as God's acts become the paradigms by which our own ideals are formed and our own acting inspired.

Reflection of this kind on the symbol of divine action might be described as placing it within the sphere of final rather than of efficient causation. God affects the world not by the manipulation of events but by making it possible for men and women to glimpse his purposes of love and be inspired by that vision. To understand the symbol in such terms is not to diminish the seriousness with which the language of 'action' is being taken. For the inspiration of goals, or ideals, and the vision of genuinely new possibilities are powerful forms of action; they are of vital importance in determining how people act and how the world develops. At the human level the most mature and fully personal form of action between persons is when one person lets another see what are his or her deepest aims and motives in a way which leads the other freely to adopt them for himself. But we must not make the mistake of regarding even an account of this kind as constituting a direct description of how God acts. God cannot be said to have aims and motives in precisely the way that we do, nor does he disclose them to us in the way that we do to one another. In speaking of God, the symbolic language cannot be replaced by a more direct, non-symbolic account. The task of theological reflection is to explore ways in which the symbol may or may not appropriately be understood. Where such exploration seeks the meaning of divine action in terms of efficient causation, however skilfully and sophisticatedly the task is undertaken it is liable to give rise to a feeling of anxiety that perhaps the symbol does not point in the direction of any acceptable meaning at all. My claim is that to look rather in the direction of final causation may be an important step towards the overcoming of that sense of anxiety.

So far I have been speaking in very general terms. I have been suggesting a framework of interpretation with which to seek to make sense of the Christian conviction of the personal, living and active God. The test will come in seeing how well such an approach enables us to understand those aspects of divine action that are central to Christian faith. And nothing is more

universality'.[2] The similarity between this and forms of the language of faith, particularly sacramental language, is obvious and important. The distinctive characteristic of the metaphoric imagination is to bring together heterogeneous elements into an organic unity, in a way that does not simply do away with the original difference but is capable of giving rise to radical novelty.[3] There is a parallel here to the way in which the religious use of the image or symbol unites things that the analytic mind chooses to distinguish. At times this uniting of disparate elements by means of a single image may take the form of asserting a paradoxical identity between them. And this may be more than a trick of fancy or an attention-catching device. 'A poet,' writes Wheelwright, 'tries not merely to startle through paradox but *to express truth through paradox*'.[4]

Paradoxes of a comparable kind are also a marked feature of religious life and expression. They strike us with particular force when we meet with them in so-called primitive religions, whose whole background and culture are different from our own. Anthropologists, in their studies of such religions, account for them in differing ways. One way has been to regard them as contraventions of the law of contradiction and to ascribe them to a pre-logical way of thinking. Such an approach is particularly linked with the name of Lévy-Bruhl, though his last writings include important qualifications of such a description. In them he plays down the aspect of pre-logical thinking or 'contradiction in the rigorous sense of the term'. His stress is rather on an idea of mystical participation, which may involve the idea 'of incompatibility in the physical sense, but not of logical absurdity'.[5] What he emphasizes is a duality of vision, characteristic of religious life as far back as we can trace it. 'As far as we are permitted to go back into observable primitive societies . . . man has had the revelation that the reality is such as he sees it and at the same time there exists another reality, or better said, that the reality given to him is at one and the same time what it is and other than what it is.'[6] Moreover, while still maintaining the difference between the mentality of 'primitive peoples' and our own societies, he also recognizes important elements in common between the two.[7]

Others have tried to say more by way of explanation of the strangely paradoxical assertions that we encounter. A famous example is Evans-Pritchard's account of Nuer Religion, in which he describes how the Nuer say of rain or a crocodile or a fetish bundle that it is Spirit or is God. On the face of it, these 'statements implying identity are very firm and unambiguous'.[8] But Evans-Pritchard argues that it is a mistake to regard them as affirming a straightforward identity. Careful reflection on their usage shows that 'the "is" does not in all instances have the same connotation'. He distinguishes an 'elliptical' use, where the object apparently identified with Spirit is really an instrument of Spirit; a 'symbolical' use, where the object represents Spirit for certain people in certain contexts in which its other characteristics are ignored; and a use which comes nearer to but still falls short of strict identity.[9] In all these cases Evans-Pritchard is concerned with *prima facie* affirmations of identity between Spirit and a material object. But he points also to similar affirmations of identity between two material objects, such as 'this cucumber is an ox', when one is being used to replace or represent the other in a ritual context. This, too, he sees, as not affirming a strict identity, but only a symbolic one.[10]

Others have gone much further in offering accounts that rationalize and play down the significance of such apparently paradoxical statements. But such accounts never seem to do justice to what the religious language is seeking to convey. 'The "Lévy-Bruhlian" character of religious thought', claims Skorupski, 'remains unaccounted for by intellectualism.'[11] And even Evans-Pritchard comes under criticism from Skorupski for tending to account for Nuer language and practice instead of providing an elucidation of them.[12]

Prima facie identity statements of this kind are not a feature only of 'primitive religions'. They are to be found in Christianity

33

too. Since most theologians are themselves Christians, they are inclined to give a more sympathetic interpretation of such language than were some at least of the earlier anthropologists in their descriptions of the religion of peoples from an alien and less sophisticated culture than their own. But if Evans-Pritchard's careful discrimination of the nuances in Nuer linguistic usage can be regarded as failing to catch the full flavour of what is being expressed there, so too the analytically trained theologian may not be the best person to evaluate such language in its Christian context. As the heavy hand of the literary critic may often succeed only in dulling the edge of poetry, however good his or her intentions, so the theologian may not find it easy to draw out the significance of these striking forms of religious language.

So in this chapter I propose to take four examples of Christian religious affirmations that fall broadly under the heading of *prima facie* identity statements. They are not all of the same form, but they share at least three things in common. Explicitly or implicitly they all appear to involve a striking form of identity claim. Each can be seen as of central importance for a particular area of Christian theology and piety. Each is capable of being misconstrued in a way that can give rise to false corollaries and unreal problems. And I begin with the one that stands closest to the kind of example that has particularly attracted the attention of the anthropologist.

1. *This is my body*

There are few sayings in Christian history over which so much blood has been spilt. On the face of it, it is as absurd an affirmation as that of the Nuer that the cucumber they are offering in sacrifice is an ox. To some Christians even the suggestion of such a parallel will seem unworthy, not to say offensive. It is not intended as more than a starting-point of reflection, but as such it can be helpful. It is a reminder how readily and how widely such strange forms of copular predication appear in ritual con-

34

texts. It does not fall precisely into either of Evans-Pritchard's types of symbolic identity, since it is neither straightforwardly an identification of bread with Spirit nor of bread and physical body as two material objects. This ambivalence complicates the story of its interpretation.

Anthropologists interpreting this kind of statement from 'primitive religions' have tended to take one of two courses. Either they have stressed the direct and literal nature of the apparent identity claim, in which case they have attributed it to a primitive, pre-logical form of thought; or else they have argued that the link between the two was really understood in a less stark and unqualified form than the wording would seem to imply. The best of them, as we have seen, are far from satisfied with the adequacy of either extreme in interpretation, but the tendency to move in one or other of these directions is clear enough. It is therefore a matter worthy of note that the main stream of Christian reflection on the eucharist and on the meaning of the words 'this is my body' has not developed in the way that such approaches might have led one to expect. Mary Douglas quotes these words from the Papal Encyclical *Mysterium Fidei* (1965): 'Nor is it right to treat of the mystery of transubstantiation without mentioning the marvellous change of the whole of the bread's substance into Christ's body and the whole of the wine's substance into his blood . . . and thereby to make these changes into nothing but a "trans-signification".' And she goes on to comment: 'Here is a doctrine as uncompromising as any West African fetishist's that the deity is located in a specific object, place and time and under control of a specific formula.'[13] And John Skorupski cites words of W. J. O'Shea to the effect that 'the bread becomes the body of Christ, the same body which he took of Mary, and which hung upon the cross'.[14] In the light of evidence of that kind, Skorupski concludes that the church accepts the impossibility of 'showing how a strict supernatural mystery, such as the doctrine of the Eucharist . . . can avoid strictly logical incoherence. Nevertheless,' he goes on, 'it regards such doctrines as literally – and certainly not metaphorically or symbolically – true.'[15]

Mary Douglas regards her comparison of the Papal Encyclical with primitive religions as a commendation of its teaching as something much to be preferred to those watered-down expressions of the faith which appeal to 'open-minded English teachers' with 'their impoverished symbolic perception';[16] and Skorupski sees the existence of 'a reflectively intellectual and penetratingly logical tradition which, far from speedily eliminating the . . . paradoxes, gives them an official epistemological status of their own'[17] as important evidence against those intellectualist accounts of religion, which tend to explain such paradoxes away. Not all Roman Catholics would acknowledge an account of their tradition which stressed the acceptance of logical incoherence as firmly as Skorupski does. Nevertheless it is clearly true that that tradition does lay stress, particularly at a popular level, on the mysterious and paradoxical character of the transformation of the elements. But even though the persistence of this tradition may be, as Skorupski affirms, an important pointer to the inadequacy of other available explanations, that need not involve acceptance of it in precisely the form in which it presents itself. Nor indeed is the Catholic tradition the only reflective tradition about the significance of the eucharist. We need to consider further its origins and development before determining how this remarkable form of Christian language is best understood.

The meaning of the words in their original use at the Last Supper has been endlessly discussed. It is clear that behind what Jesus did and said there was a rich tradition of Jewish practice and symbolism. But such background, though important, was not decisive for Jesus' meaning. John Baker cautiously sums up an article on 'The "Institution Narratives" and the Christian Eucharist' by saying:

It would seem that in the institution Jesus himself, inspired

36

though he may have been at the level of creative imagination by the great festival in which he and his friends were taking part, did not tie himself down nor seek to tie them down to any particular Old Testament interpretation of what he was doing – and *a fortiori* he did not tie us.[18]

Early Christian usage certainly treats the language in a straightforwardly realistic way. But the most realistic language stands side by side in the same authors with more spiritualizing or symbolic language. Thus the sixth chapter of St John's Gospel can speak of the necessity of eating Christ's flesh in a way that puzzles and offends the Jews, and in almost the same breath assert that 'it is the Spirit that gives life, the flesh is of no avail'.[19] This is still more clearly marked in the writings of the early Fathers, where symbolic and realistic language stand together without any sense of strain. They speak of the bread simply as 'Christ's body' or as the 'figure' or 'antitype' of his body without any indication of intended difference in meaning.[20] The more developed and theoretical accounts of the nature of the change involved, which culminate in the mediaeval doctrine of transubstantiation, arise from a desire to stress that a real union of God and man is effected through the sacramental action and the reception of the elements. But explanations of that kind are always liable to isolate the thing that they are trying to explain and thereby remove it from the one context in which it is capable of being properly understood. It was partly to overcome that weakness that a number of Roman Catholic scholars in recent years developed the concept of 'trans-signification', of which the Papal Encyclical, *Mysterium Fidei*, spoke with such caution.[21] For Schillebeeckx, who is the outstanding exponent of these ideas, a change of substance is a change at the deepest level of reality. It is not Christ's being present in some matter-of-fact sense of 'being there' that is involved, but his being there for believers in a personal way.[22] Changes of meaning are more radical than physical changes and are not dependent on them. It is a new establishment of meaning that is at the heart of the change to the bread and wine.[23]

Schillebeeckx, and other Roman Catholic theologians who follow a similar line of interpretation, tend to insist that their ideas do not involve any departure from earlier teaching about transubstantiation and its stress on the reality of the conversion of the elements. I would prefer to emphasize that the difference of conceptuality involved can help to free us constructively from the misleading puzzles and perplexities into which that doctrine seems inevitably to lead.

It was anxieties of that kind that led to the last minute introduction of the Black Rubric into the 1552 Prayer Book, with its explanatory note that kneeling to receive communion implied no adoration of 'any real and essential presence there being of Christ's natural flesh and blood'. But however justified such a reaction to mediaeval doctrine and practice may have been, it makes its point in so negative a way that it can only serve to weaken the positive religious power of the symbols being used.[24] Another Reformation rite goes further and does not merely include a cautionary rubric in the order of worship but actually requires the congregation to pray: 'Send down, O Lord, thy blessing upon this Sacrament, that it may be unto us the effectual exhibitive instrument of the Lord Jesus.'[25] The language of theology has here forgotten its secondary role and has usurped the place of the language of faith. Whatever one's evaluation of the theology as theology, the final outcome as a vehicle of worship is unqualified disaster.

But the approach in terms of trans-signification or establishment of new meaning can make the same point in a more constructive way. It can remove the mystification without diminishing the proper sense of mystery. It renders unnecessary the admission of a special form of logical incoherence, or the invention of a special set of epistemological rules. For it sees the identification of bread and body as the focal centre in the establishment of a rich pattern of shared meaning. And that pattern of shared meaning has the dual character of disclosure and creativity that we considered in relation to biblical imagery in the previous chapter. Schillebeeckx emphasizes that when bread and wine were first used at the Last Supper, there is a sense in which they were already more than bare bread and wine. They had already been given a rich meaning by a long tradition of human symbolic activity. They had been used to express human fellowship through the shared meal, to symbolize God's gift of life in the worship of the natural religions, and to play a role in the historical recollection that was a special feature of Jewish festivals.[26] In all these cases, the symbolic use of bread and wine disclosed a basic reality of human life as given by God but also served to construct a particular way of apprehending and living that reality. So in the eucharist, bread and wine are used to express and to effect a fuller and more specific apprehension of God's presence as redeeming love made known in Jesus Christ. They disclose the reality of God's presence and create a particular way in which it can be apprehended and lived. So, far from weakening the power of the symbols, such an approach to their significance strengthens and extends that power.

2. *You are the body of Christ*

Turning at this point to the second of our *prima facie* identity statements involves no sharp break in the continuity of the discussion. For the concept of the church as the body of Christ does not belong to a distinct or separate area of belief. It is one that is frequently and powerfully combined with reflection on the eucharist. Augustine, for example, in a much-quoted sermon, draws on Paul's words, 'you are the body of Christ', to show that 'it is the mystery of yourselves that is placed on the table'.[27] The bread–body of the eucharist is not that of the divine Son or the incarnate Jesus alone; it is at the same time the self-offering of the whole Christian community as well. Such an interweaving of images enables a form of worship that is both rich in the variety of its associations and powerful in the concreteness of their integration.

Since the two phrases belong so closely together in Christian life and thought, it is natural to seek our understanding of this second affirmation in terms of imagery and symbolism of the same kind that we have used in the earlier instance. It is, in fact, less common to find writers insisting on the literal character of the apparent identity claim implicit in the words 'you are the body of Christ' than it is in the case of the grammatically similar words 'this is my body'. But such claims are made, and made by those who would want to stress as strongly as I have done the interweaving of the eucharistic and ecclesiological uses of the phrase 'body of Christ'. Thus Eric Mascall writes:

> It is not a mere metaphor, but the literal truth, that the Church is the Body of Christ. Christ has only one Body, that which he took from his mother, the Virgin Mary, but that Body exists under various modes. As a natural Body it was seen on earth, hung on the Cross, rose in glory on the first Easter Day and was taken into heaven in the Ascension; as a mystical Body it appeared on earth on the first Whitsunday and we know it as the Holy Catholic Church; as a sacramental Body it becomes present on our altars at every Eucharist when, by the operation of the Holy Ghost and the priestly act of Christ, bread and wine are transformed into, and made one with, the glorified Body which is in heaven.[28]

Mascall's detailed spelling out of a literal sense in which the church is the body of Christ raises a number of different problems. But the basic question is: What grounds are there for regarding the predication as a literal one in the first place?

The direct statement, 'you are the body of Christ', comes from Paul's first letter to the Corinthians (12.27). Paul's language is direct and unqualified. That fact in itself could never be decisive. Its significance is further weakened by the presence of other affirmations of precisely the same grammatical structure elsewhere in the same epistle: 'you are God's building' (I Cor. 3.9) and 'God's temple' (I Cor. 3.16).

But the directness of the language certainly needs to be taken seriously. We need to ask what it implies about each term of the affirmation. The 'you' to whom Paul refers is the local Corinthian church, that same group of people whom he castigates earlier in the epistle and of whom he says: 'you are carnal' (I Cor. 3.3–4). To insist that the words apply to the local Corinthian church is not, of course, to suggest that they apply to them exclusively. But it is important to recognize that it is not some idealized concept of an invisible church universal that Paul has in mind, but the actual group of wayward Christians who made up the Christian community at Corinth.[29] And what of 'body'? The language is certainly striking. The metaphor is a living one in a way that the use of the word 'body' to refer to some social entity is not for us today. Moreover it is not the general idea of a body but specifically the body of Christ of which Paul speaks. Considerations of these kinds led J. A. T. Robinson to declare:

> It is almost impossible to exaggerate the materialism and crudity of Paul's doctrine of the Church as literally now the resurrection *body* of Christ. The language of 'membership' of a body corporate has become so trite that the idea that the individual can be a 'member' has ceased to be offensive. The force of Paul's words can to-day perhaps be got by paraphrasing: 'Ye are the body of Christ and severally membranes thereof' (I Cor. 12.27). The body that he has in mind is as concrete and as singular as the body of the Incarnation.[30]

But if it be almost impossible to exaggerate the realism of Paul's language, Robinson has certainly succeeded in achieving the almost impossible. The use of the word 'literally' is as unjustified for him in this context as an exgete, as I believe it to be for Mascall as a theologian. We have already pointed to the comparable usage of a wide range of other images of the church which cannot all be taken literally. If Colossians and Ephesians are regarded as Pauline, as Robinson does regard them,[31] the case is clearer still. For while in I Corinthians the head is just one of the members of the body (I Cor. 12.21), in Colossians and Ephesians Christ is specifically identified as the head (Col. 1.18; 2.19; Eph. 1.22; 4.15). One cannot treat both sets of references in the literal or realistic way that Robinson advocates.[32]

But as we have seen in our citation from Mascall, this view has been maintained not only as an issue of Pauline exegesis but also as a constituent element in subsequent Christian theology. It ought not to be regarded as merely a regrettable piece of grammatical misclassification; it is religiously dangerous as well. And the danger is widely recognized today, not only by radical protestant opponents of any form of institutional church life, but by Roman Catholics and others of a generally catholic tradition as well. Thus Avery Dulles declares that 'the designation of the church as the Body of Christ is in danger of leading to an unhealthy divinization of the church. It seems to suggest the erroneous position . . . that the church is one organism together with its head, and the union is therefore a biological and hypostatic one'.[33] And Michael Schmaus argues that 'the image of the People of God is a necessary complement to that of the Body of Christ in order to show clearly the differences between Christ and the Church as a society of the believing faithful, so that the Church is not absorbed in a mystical identity with the existence of Christ'.[34]

But as in the case of the eucharist, so here too it is important to be able to make such a criticism in a way that does not destroy the vigour of the symbol. This is something of which Dulles, and other such writers, are fully aware. And the essential prerequisite for so doing is to free ourselves from talk of 'mere metaphor' and to recognize the role of metaphor as disclosing and creating reality. For to speak of the church as the body of Christ gives expression within a single image to two

fundamental realities of Christian life. In the first place it points
to an intimacy of relationship to God to be found in the life of
the Christian community. The form of the language suggests an
understanding of that relationship in terms of personal identity.
Christians are the body of Christ. But such language cannot be
treated as a straightforward description of the relationship.
Christians are also spoken of as standing to God as sons to a
father or servants to a master. Identity language is a valuable
supplement to such interpersonal language, because of the way
it speaks of the inwardness of our relation to God which is never
simply a relation to one who stands over against us as an other
than ourselves. But it speaks at the same time with equal effectiveness of another reality. Our relationship to God as Christians
is no private or individual matter. It is inescapably bound up
with our relationship with our fellows. Our human inter-
dependence is essential to the establishment of a Christian
relationship to God and contributes to its distinctive character.
Clement Webb, indeed, sees the early Christians' understanding of the church as the body of Christ as of vital importance for
their conception of God. It was, he argues, the way in which
their common life was so intimately bound up with their apprehension of God through Christ that gave rise to a fully personal
conception of God. The reason that early Christian conception
of God was so distinctively personal in character was, he argues,
'not because it was a conception of him as an individual conscious being (Aristotle's conception of God was that), but because it recognized in the *personal* relations of fellow-Christians
to one another a relation to him who said, "Inasmuch as ye
have done it to the least of these my brethren ye did it unto
me" '.[35]

3. *Inasmuch as you have done it to the least of these my brethren, you did
   it unto me*

Those words constitute the third putative identity claim that
I want to consider. It is not expressed with the same directness

43

as the two we have considered so far. In Evans-Pritchard's classification, it belongs most naturally to the elliptical or instrumental form of identity claim. We would not therefore expect to find this affirmation understood with the same degree of realism that we have met in some of the interpretations of the words 'you are the body of Christ'. Indeed, it is not only the difference in linguistic form that is significant here. It would be a much more difficult thing to insist on a strongly realistic meaning to this affirmation with its individual reference than where the reference is to the body as a whole. It is a familiar characteristic of social experience that people are often inclined to make extravagant claims for the social entity to which they belong – be it class or nation or race – of a kind that they would not dream of making about any individual member of that group. Nevertheless, the words do seem to imply some form of identity claim. What is done to the least of his brethren is to be regarded as done to the Son of Man or the King of the gospel story. And it is not just an arbitrary fiction; to see it that way is to see the deepest truth of the matter. The identity cannot be directly affirmed, but nor can it be straightforwardly denied. As Richard Niebuhr puts it, 'the needy companion is not wholly other than Christ, though he is not Christ himself'.[36]

But who is 'the needy companion' of the story? Webb, as we have seen, applies the saying to the relation of Christians to one another. More commonly it is given a wider reference in attempts to elicit from Christians a universal compassion. In a Policy Statement on Christian Aid and World Development, the British Council of Churches appealed to it to reinforce the universal claim of suffering humanity on the care and compassion of Christians. 'In every human being in need,' the statement declared, 'we are confronted by Jesus Christ himself and . . . if we deny Him in this encounter we cannot belong to him at all.'[37] The allusion to the Matthaean parable, though not explicit, is clear enough. In the brief credal statements and their explanations with which Karl Rahner concludes his *Foundations of Christian Faith*,[38] it is given a wider reference still. Matthew 25 is the one passage of scripture to which he refers directly. In it he finds evidence to support his conviction 'that the entire salvific relationship between man and God and between man and Christ is already found implicitly in a radical love for one's neighbour realised in practice'.[39]

In these three writings we see the text applied to the relation of Christians to one another, the relation of Christians to other human beings irrespective of their faith, and to the relation of men and women to one another whoever they may be. Yet it is unlikely that any of those three interpretations can claim to be giving the original intention of the story in St Matthew's gospel. The two preceding parables in Matthew 25 (the parables of the wise and foolish virgins and of the talents) are directed to the question of the judgment to be faced by Christians. The tory of the sheep and the goats describes the judgment of the 'nations' or 'Gentiles', and the criterion of judgment for them is how they have treated the least of Christ's brethren. The intention of the story in that context is almost certainly to teach that the non-Christian world will be judged on the basis of how it has treated the despised Christian community. The original reference seems therefore to have been to the relation of non-Christians to Christians – the one relationship not included in the three interpretations I have quoted.

How we should evaluate the story, if we accept that as its original intention, does not affect our present discussion. Such a reading of it does not remove the implicit identity claim, though it does restrict it to the Christian church. Thus, though the context and teaching of the story is very different from that involved in designating the church as the body of Christ, the quasi-identity claim would have the same scope in both cases. But Christian theology is not and should not be confined to reasserting simply the original intentions of the New Testament writings. Parables, or stories like that of the sheep and the goats, may properly be seen as material for imaginative reflection.

And when understood in that way, the use to which the story is put in the passages quoted from the British Council of Churches and from Karl Rahner may prove to be both justified and of value.

Christians traditionally speak of love of God and love of neighbour as the two great commandments of Christ. St Luke in fact ascribes this bringing together of those two commands, each of which appears separately within the Old Testament, not to Jesus himself but to the lawyer with whom he is discussing. And he follows that account with the parable of the Good Samaritan, thus making the primary contribution of Jesus an insistence that the 'neighbour' is not to be restricted to fellow-Israelite or fellow-disciple but means fellow-human being, even, indeed especially, one's enemy.[40]

Nor does St Luke (unlike St Matthew or St Mark) speak of love of God and love of neighbour as two commandments; in his gospel they simply stand together as parts of one single comprehensive statement of what the law requires. And other writings in the New Testament go even further in stressing the interconnectedness of the two. The first epistle of St John declares that 'if any one says "I love God" and hates his brother, he is a liar; for he who does not love his brother whom he has seen, cannot love God whom he has not seen' (I John 4.20). The author is not arguing that love of God is a more difficult activity than loving one's neighbours; he is rather insisting that the two are so bound up with one another that it is logically impossible to do one without the other. It is not like saying 'if you can't manage whist, it is no use trying to learn to play bridge'; it is more like saying 'if you won't marry me, you can't love me'. The epistle, it is true, confines itself exclusively to the relation between the love of God and love of the brother or fellow-Christian. It is an extension, but I would claim a legitimate extension, to postulate a similar relation between love of God and love of neighbour, understood in the sense indicated by the parable of the Good Samaritan.

Considerations of this kind do seem to me to justify the extended use to which the Matthaean story is so frequently put. But even if justified, is it of any significance? The form of identity is certainly no strict identity. To treat it as such and so regard love of neighbour as coterminous with and indistinguishable from love of God is dangerously misleading. But the form in which the identity is asserted is a powerful expression of the inseparability of the two and it provides a good illustration of one of the primary characteristics of Christian ethics.

For what is distinctive in Christian ethics is not that it imposes new or different obligations which are not already binding on human beings as human beings. However much Christian revelation may have contributed historically to the grasping of new moral insights, those insights have still had to be recognized, assessed and applied by the ordinary methods of ethical reflection. The distinctive character of Christian ethics lies not in the difference of its moral demands but in the way in which it sets them within the context of a particular vision. Gerard Hughes argues cogently for the thesis that 'the Christian faith, while not adding any substantive content to our moral knowledge or arguments, nevertheless provides a stimulus, a context and a motivation'.[41] And it is precisely that that is conveyed by the words 'in as much as you did it unto one of the least of these my brethren, you did it unto me'. We have a duty to our fellowmen and women in need by virtue of our common humanity. We do not have a different duty to them, if we come to see that in fulfilling or neglecting that duty we are doing or failing to do it to Christ. But the moral command is powerfully reinforced by being imaginatively integrated into a religious vision. It ceases to be simply a formal, if categorical, imperative and is transmuted into an integral part of a response of personal love.

Such an integrated vision lends itself more naturally to expression in imaginative writing than to theological analysis. And it is in the former vein that it has mainly been developed in Christian history. A typical example is Tolstoi's short story 'Where

Love is there God is also'.[42] The cobbler, Martin Avdéitch, has been reading the gospels and hears a voice assuring him that Christ will come to him on the next day. It is only when the day is over and the promise apparently unfulfilled that he comes to see it has in fact been fulfilled in the persons of the old man and the destitute young woman with her baby whom he has befriended and helped in the course of the day. But to acknowledge that that is the vein in which the idea is most naturally developed is not to denigrate its importance; it is not to imply that it is a matter of merely subjective and sentimental fancy, 'pure play of the artistic imagination'. We have once again to do with that which 'partly discloses and partly creates hitherto unknown, unguessed aspects of What Is'. For it is an imaginative construction which can make us see and experience our neighbour in a new way. But it is not pure creation. For it helps to disclose an inexpressible and mysterious truth about God's relation to men and women, created in his own image. For God's self-identification in love with his creation, which is yet also emphatically other than himself, is something that cannot be directly described or precisely defined in words; it is best conveyed by that vision which springs out of the words 'inasmuch as you did it unto one of the least of these my brethren, you did it unto me'.

We have been looking at three basic Christian affirmations, each simple in form but profound in meaning. They have led us into some central concerns of Christian ethics, ecclesiology and sacramental thought. They are interrelated not only in form, but in substance. They constitute, as it were, three concentric circles. They offer a pattern of profound symbolism whereby we can articulate the conviction that in the fundamental realities of our life we have to do very directly with God himself. In the outer circles we have our relations with our fellow human beings. This is never a purely private matter between us and them, of finite and delimited extent. It has always a transcendent dimension. What we do to them, we do to God. In the next circle moving inwards we have our relation with those who share our Christian allegiance. Since Christian faith in God is part of an interpretation of life that can only arise in an inter-subjective context, the common life of believers is not just a corollary of such a faith; it is a constitutive part of it. Moving further in, we have the sacramental expression which is the focus of that shared meaning and shared experience of the Christian community. So in each of these three areas we can appropriately speak of that which we experience directly – our fellow human being in need, our fellow Christian, the sacramental bread and wine – as embodying the reality that we experience in and through them. Each in its own way is the body of Christ. But our Hamlet remains as yet without its prince of Denmark. For further in towards the centre of these concentric circles stands the figure of Christ himself. Our faith language speaks of what we do to others as done to *Christ* and of church and sacrament as the body of *Christ*. But I have spoken of their meaning in terms of our relationship with God. Implicit in such treatment is yet another and more fundamental *prima facie* identity claim – between Christ and God. What form of identity claim is it that we have to do with at the heart of our concentric circles?

4. *'I and my Father are one': 'He who has seen me has seen the Father'* *(John 10.30; 14.9)*

In discussion of the relation between Christ and God, theologians are much more inclined to insist on a strict sense of identity than they are in those other areas of theology that we have considered so far. Moreover, the claim has a much broader base than in those other spheres. There is no single statement of identity in scripture that plays as crucial a role here as did the texts that have been at the centre of our earlier discussions. The two quotations at the heading of this section have not been as vital for christology as the words of institution have been for eucharistic theology. Nevertheless, they do represent significant identity claims of the two types with which we have become

49

familiar, the one direct and the other of a more indirect or instrumental kind. And they have played an important role, often in conjunction with one another, in the history of doctrine.

'Jesus', says one modern writer, 'was metaphysically not metaphorically one with Almighty God.'[43] That is precisely the contrast to which we are accustomed. Yet even for so strongly conservative a writer as Michael Green, the identity is not unqualified. 'It would be ridiculous,' he writes, 'to imagine that Jesus is God *tout simple*.'[44] That the identity required some kind of qualification has been recognized from the earliest days of Christian history. According to Tertullian at the beginning of the third century, some Christians of his day, the so-called 'monarchians', did maintain the total identity of the Father and Christ, using as their primary evidence the two Johannine texts at the head of this section. Tertullian submits their case to a wide range of criticisms. If full personal identity were intended by the words 'I and my Father are one', he argues, the verb would have to be in the singular and the final word, 'one', would need to be masculine, not neuter as it is in Greek.[45] But it is doubtful whether even the monarchians were claiming an unqualified identity between *Jesus* and God. We cannot reconstruct their beliefs with certainty, but it seems most probable that, while claiming total identity between the Father and Christ, they still allowed for some qualification in the identity between that Father-Christ and the figure of Jesus.[46]

But the question of who could offer the more convincing exegesis of the direct forms of apparent identity claim to be found in scripture was not the heart of the matter. The more indirect forms of claim were the more significant. To see Jesus is to see the Father; to receive Jesus is to receive the one who sent him; Jesus pronounces forgiveness in a way that belongs only to God; the judgment-seat before which we must all stand can equally well be described as the judgment-seat of God or the judgment-seat of Christ.[47] And so down the ages the conviction has been maintained: if Jesus is not God, he cannot save; if Jesus is not God, he cannot reveal. It runs through from Athanasius' insistence that only a Christ who is in himself fully divine, of one substance with the Father, can be man's saviour, to Barth's insistence that, if there is any real revelation of God at all, then 'we must understand that this subject, God, the Revealer, is identical with His act in revelation'.[48]

So the church has developed and insisted on a sense of identity which is as strong a sense of identity as is conceivable short of identity *tout simple*. And in doing so it has had to develop, as in eucharistic thought, a special logic for describing the status of those paradoxes that it cannot understand but is unwilling to eliminate. And it has had to do so on two fronts. In trinitarian theology it speaks of a unique kind of relationship, of persons who are identical with one another in every respect apart from the differences of the relationships that they have to each other. And in christology it has to speak of the unmixed but inseparable unity of the fully divine and fully human in a single person.

In the light of our earlier review of the place of imagery and paradox, of symbolic language and concrete universals in poetry and in religious usage, the question arises inescapably: is this the only fitting way, is it the most fitting way in which to understand these affirmations that lie at the heart of the Christian's faith language? We have seen how some apparently straightforward identity claims are best understood in an instrumental or symbolic sense. The possibility of an interpretation along those lines in this case also deserves to be seriously explored.

In the synoptic records of the ministry of Jesus, one story stands out as depicting the supra-human character of Jesus and his mission in a particularly transparent way. That story is the story of the transfiguration. Other stories, like the feeding of the five thousand or the raising of the widow of Nain's son, may involve more striking miraculous powers. But what is distinctive about the story of the transfiguration is that the whole scenario

51

is strange; it seems to belong to another order of being which we are not sure whether to call an unreal, dreamlike state or a more than real divine order. It has more in common with nativity stories about the Magi following their star or the shepherds communing with angels in the fields, and with post-resurrection stories where Jesus appears through closed doors and is only half recognizable on the Emmaus road, than with the other stories of the main period of the ministry. Some scholars have indeed been led by such similarities to treat it as a misplaced resurrection story. Such a suggestion cannot be taken beyond the stage of sheer conjecture. The importance of such reflections is not in what they say about the earlier history of the story but in what they suggest for its subsequent inter-pretation. It is not so much one additional incident to be added to the various stories of the ministry of Jesus, but rather an invitation to the reader to see that whole story in a particular light. Like the parables, it stands as a challenge to those who 'look and look but never see' (Matt. 13.14). It says: when you look at this man do you not see the vision? Do you not see the glory?

The Fourth Gospel contains no record of the transfiguration. For the Fourth Evangelist, the fundamental character of the whole gospel story is that in it we behold the 'glory, the glory as of the only-begotten of the Father'. For him the whole gospel is a transfiguration story. It is the story of a real man, a man of flesh and blood who lived and died in Palestine; but the story is told from start to finish at a level of narration similar to that which pervades the transfiguration story. Treat it in any other light and the man of flesh and blood, of whom the author clearly wishes to speak, disappears and becomes an unreal, docetic figure who only prays to impress the bystanders (John 11.42) and who has only to speak to send a detachment of soldiers falling to the ground (John 18.6). Now it is in this gospel that the most direct claims of identity between Jesus and God or between the Son and the Father are to be found. And, as I have argued elsewhere,[49] it is those claims occurring within this gospel that have played a particularly important part in the church's insistence on a direct identification between Jesus and God in orthodox theology. But is the understanding of the gospel on which that insistence has been based one that is true to the character of the gospel itself? As I read the gospel, what it says to me is essentially what the transfiguration story says: in the light of this man's story do you not see the vision? Does it not lead you to a new awareness of God's glory in the world and of the transformation of human life that that can bring?

4

Jesus and the Way of Faith

How then do I read the story of Jesus? And what is the nature of the vision to which it gives rise?

There have been times when Christians have been able to read the story oblivious of any distance between history and text, between the happenings and the records. That is no longer possible. I cannot read the story without recognizing that there are differences between what Jesus of Nazareth did and said in Palestine, and the stories of him that the evangelists record. Both matter to me as I come to the gospels as a source of faith. If Christians are serious when they speak of the word made flesh in Jesus and of the centrality of Jesus for their faith, they cannot be unconcerned to know what can be known of him as a historical person. But there is no way to such knowledge that bypasses the work of the historical scholar. Such work is inevitably tentative in character, and the 'historical Jesus' of one scholar may be very different from the 'historical Jesus' of another. Frustratingly uncertain though their reconstructions may be, I cannot simply ignore them if my concern is with the story of *Jesus*. But the concern of the person of faith is not identical with the concern of the historian. If my concern is with the significance of Jesus for faith, it is also with the *story* of Jesus, with what he meant for the faith of the earliest Christians as we see that reflected in the way the evangelists tell his story.

It is not unusual to read historical records with this kind of stereoscopic vision – with one eye on the subject-matter of the narration and one eye on what the records reveal of the attitudes and convictions of the narrator. The scholar is primarily concerned to distinguish; the man or woman of faith seeks to integrate them, for his concern is with the vision of faith to which the figure of Jesus gives rise. Such a concern is no artificial addition imposed on the material. We are not taking hold of chronicles written with a narrowly historical purpose and wresting them to some alien use. Indeed, it was an intrinsic part of the ministry of Jesus himself to elicit from those who heard him a response of faith; and it was certainly integral to the writing of the early Christian records about him. But the fact that we come to the records of Jesus with this concern gives rise to another factor that influences our reading of the story. We come to it aware of the fact that the story has been the occasion of faith throughout the centuries that separate the writing of the gospels from our own time, and aware also of the varied ways in which it has fulfilled that role. The long history of how the gospels have been read and understood in the life of the church inevitably affects the way in which we approach them now. But since our concern is for a vision of faith that will be genuinely our own, our reading of the story will be even more influenced by what speaks to us, by what appears to us to constitute a possible way of faith today. All reading of history is reading from the standpoint of particular interests and presuppositions. These contribute to what we find, though they in their turn may also be challenged and modified by it. So when I come to the records of Jesus within the context of the life of faith, I come not simply as a historian desiring to reconstruct a picture of Jesus as he once was; nor do I come simply as a reader interested to rediscover the faith of the early disciples. Those concerns are necessary elements in my reading of the story, but they do not make up the whole. I seek to let what I learn by those means interact with my own experience and ask: how do I see this Jesus, and how does seeing him lead me to see the Father?

First and foremost I see him as one for whom God is an all-encompassing reality. All the hairs of our heads are numbered; and not a sparrow falls to the ground without the Father (Matt. 10.29f.). This sense of God's all-pervading presence he seeks to kindle in his hearers by appeal to the imagination through parable and aphorism. Its impact is both reassuring and disturbing. Jesus himself appears as having an unassailable confidence in God and in his own relation to him. Yet what that meant for him in practice was not something that came to him easily, nor was it something lightly carried out, as the stories of the temptation, of Gethsemane[1] and the cry of dereliction on the cross so vividly express. So, too, for his hearers. The sinner may know himself forgiven and the outcast an accepted and treasured member of God's people. But obedience to God may involve the renunciation of all human ties and of all worldly security, for those who take Jesus at his word as much as for Jesus himself. To be a follower is to be a follower in the way of the cross.

I have begun my picture in general terms with the spatial imagery of God's all-pervading presence. But the peculiar dynamic of the message of Jesus lay rather in its specific character and in the temporal insistence on the imminence of the coming of the rule, or kingdom, of God. In many ways Jesus stood within the tradition of the ancient prophets: the directness of his delivery of God's word; the call to repentance; the challenge to the religious authorities of his day; the combination of word and act in expression of his message. But he saw himself as something more than just another one in a prophetic succession. If John the Baptist was more than a prophet, in Jesus' own ministry one greater than John the Baptist was to be seen. The message of the book of Daniel in the second century BC, and of other apocalypses which did not find their way into the Jewish or Christian canon, had been that God would act soon and decisively to bring to a triumphant close the long process of his age-old plan for his people. When Jesus spoke of the imminent coming of God's kingdom, it was the effective establishment of the final rule of God in that sense that he was proclaiming. It was that that gave his message its urgency. It was that that made his ministry unique. It was that that lay behind the insistence that the form of people's response to Jesus was to be the criterion of their final judgment before God.

But if this expectation gave to the ministry of Jesus its distinctive force and urgency, it did not distort or narrow his message, as similar expectations have so often done in the course of human history. All ties must be subordinated to the obedience and call of God. But this shortening of the perspective of human history does not lead to a disregard for the needs of humanity. Indeed those needs are exalted to the point of challenge against the religious establishment of his day. Obedience to God was not to be identified with obedience to the law, if its requirements were interpreted in ways that conflicted with fundamental human needs. The Sabbath was made for man, not man for the Sabbath (Mark 2.27). The lawyer must see that the dictates of the law lead to the humanitarian practice of the Good Samaritan, and the rich young ruler that for him they entail parting with his possessions and giving to the poor. The characteristic of God is the generous outreach of his love, and the disciple must follow him with a forgiveness that does not prescribe whom or how often it will forgive.

We speak of these things as 'the teaching of Jesus'. But their natural setting was the market-place rather than the lecture-room. They figure within the context of an urgent proclamation of the imminence of the coming of God's kingdom. They were part of a summons to pursue a way of life that was in conflict with the ideals of many of those in positions of authority. So the ministry of Jesus gave rise to a head-on clash with the religious establishment of his day. And the outcome of that clash was the crucifixion of Jesus, the apparent falsification of his message and his hopes. But the grave of Jesus proved to be not the place of death and decay, but the womb of life and renewal. His death was perhaps foreseen by Jesus himself, and certainly soon came to be seen by his followers as something done in faithful obedience to the will of God. It proved to be a source of healing to the nations; it was the initiatory stage in a process that gave new power and universal scope to that message of God's love and forgiveness which his life and his lips had declared.

In the story the death and resurrection of Jesus belong intimately together. The meaning of one cannot be grasped in isolation from the meaning of the other. But historically the two are events of a very different kind. The resurrection is so strange an event that the historical eye of our twofold stereoscopic vision cannot focus properly upon it. What the historical eye sees is the transformation of life to which Jesus gave rise and the conviction of those who experienced it that what they were experiencing was the life of the risen Christ at work. For many Christians that transformation of life is seen as clear evidence of a supernatural historical event at its source – an 'objective' resurrection involving some kind of physical change to the body of Jesus, its coming out from the tomb and being made present on various occasions to the disciples. But, for me, an understanding of resurrection in those 'objective' terms is part of one possible reconstruction of past events rather than something essential to faith. I see the quality and continuing strength of that transformation of life as evidence not so much of what historical happenings lie behind it, but rather of the validity of the spiritual insight that it embodies. The Old Testament is a story of hopes that time and again prove to be falsified at the level of their original expectation, but are later seen as fulfilled at another, deeper level of reality.[2] The hope of God's perpetual presence in Solomon's temple was frustrated by the destruction of the temple by the Assyrians. But at another level the destruction of the temple opened the way to a fuller realization of God's presence with his people. It enabled them to learn more deeply that their God was no localized deity; he was not a God who dwelt in temples made with hands, nor was he God only of a particular land or place. He was a God who could be worshipped and called upon by exiles in a foreign land, a God whose writ and authority ran to the furthest extremities of the world. In a similar way, the hope of Jesus for the coming of God's kingdom was not fulfilled in the form that he apparently expected. Yet in a radically transformed sense that hope can be spoken of as finding fulfilment. For the seeming disaster of Jesus' death, like the disaster of the Jewish exile, was the catalyst that transformed the hope of Jesus in its immediate Palestinian Jewish form into a spiritual force of far greater range and power. In the community that derived from him, his vision of what would mark the kingdom was reaffirmed as God's will for mankind. Whatever the immediate historical occasion of that transformation, the eye of faith had come to see in Jesus the presence of God's spirit at work in unprecedented power. And it saw that work not simply as something confined to his lifetime, but as something that he was continuing to do in and through the Christian community.

So, as I read the story of Jesus, I ask questions as realistically as I can about the history; I try to understand the faith and convictions of his earliest interpreters. When I stand back from my reading and seek to respond to it as a whole, then history and interpretation combine to give rise to a vision of God in relation to the world, for which the figure of Jesus and the movement that stems from him are central. For if the action of God is best understood as 'the inspiration of goals or ideals and the vision of genuinely new possibilities',[3] then God was supremely active in Jesus and the birth of the Christian church. There is no one right way of describing the relation of God to the world that such a vision discloses. For visions of that kind, as we have seen, do not merely disclose; they also create. We must find our words from within the tradition of that symbolic language of faith which both shaped it and was shaped by it. For me, much of the language of the earliest Christians continues to give powerful expression to it. With Paul I am led to say that God was in Christ reconciling the world to himself, and that in the life of the early Christian communities God's love was poured

When Pilate said to the angry crowds, 'Behold the Man!', in the ears of Christians he was speaking more truly than he knew, for he was speaking of the second Adam. If God sent his Son into the world to redeem us, it was in order that we should be made sons too; if it was distinctive of Jesus that he could address God as 'Abba, Father', that is a distinctive mark of Christians too (Gal. 4.4–6). So in reading the story of Jesus not merely as a historian but with the concern of faith, I am seeking to see in it a way of faith for myself as a believer too. In the past, theologians have sometimes questioned whether Jesus, being co-equal Son of God incarnate, could rightly be said to have exercised the virtue of faith. 'From the very moment of conception,' argued Aquinas, 'Christ had the full vision of the very being of God. . . . Therefore he could not have had faith.'[6] All such speculations seem to me to be destructive alike of any sense of historical realism or of religious significance in the figure of Jesus. But even with the barrier of such pseudo-dogmatic smoke-screens removed, the figure of Jesus as the man of faith remains elusive. The portraits of him show features that are not easily brought together. He acts and speaks at times with a directness of authority and self-assurance that seems in danger of falling over into harshness and self-assertion. On the other hand, the pictures also convey a humility and attractiveness that is not something visible only to the eye of the pious believer, for it impinges on many an unbeliever too. Attempts at a psychological reconstruction of the character of Jesus' faith are doomed to remain highly speculative. The ways in which the acts and words of Jesus are presented in the gospels are no doubt determined partly by his understanding of his mission to proclaim the imminent kingdom of God, but also partly by the faith-stance of the different evangelists. The ambiguous nature of the material at our disposal is such that any attempted reconstruction is almost bound to be dominated by the psychological and spiritual ideals of our own day. Yet these very real difficulties should not be allowed to inhibit altogether reflection on what the figure of Jesus may have to say to us about our lives as men and women. And for me the direction in which such reflection points is one that indicates a correlation of characteristics of a kind to be met with in the lives of some saints. For sometimes there is to be seen there an inner assurance joined with a total absence of self-assertiveness; and the combination is not just a freak coexistence of opposites, for both are rooted in a single consistent attitude towards God. Thus there is a consistency between the vision of human life to which the figure of Jesus gives rise and the distinctive quality of life that marks out some outstanding Christians.

But what is the essence of this specifically Christian form of life? Here I find help in one of the earliest and most influential accounts of what it is to be Christian. Paul spoke of those who, through Jesus, had become sons of God and learned to say 'Abba, Father', as 'justified by faith'. And that language of 'justification by faith' has been a watchword of protestant Christianity down the ages. The precise meaning of the term 'justification' in Paul's thought has to be seen in relation to the problems and debates of his own day. Its rediscovery by Luther involved subtle shifts of meaning from that which it bore in its original Jewish setting of fifteen centuries earlier. Its meaning has not been constant or unchanging down the ages, but there has been continuity as well as difference. Today, the concept is widely regarded as obsolete. It 'leaves people in the Protestant churches,' says Hans Küng, 'just as cold as those in the Catholic church.'[7] So it may seem an odd place to turn in search of insight into the fundamental character of Christian living. Certainly, if we try to tie its interpretation too closely to the precise intention of past ages, the kind of reaction that Küng describes is almost inevitable. If, on the other hand, we allow for a further shift of meaning of the kind that is characteristic of any living tradition of linguistic usage, the way is open to a very different response. The phrase can properly serve to indicate that basic attitude towards God that underlies the kind of saintliness that

I am seeking to describe and that seems to me characteristically Christian.

To be justified by faith implies two things about our relationship to God. In the first place it implies that our fundamental standing in the world is determined by the acceptance of God's free and gracious love for us and not by our own merits or our own achievements. In the language of the Epistle to the Ephesians, it is by grace that we are saved through faith; and even that is not our own doing, it is the gift of God – not of works lest any man should boast (Eph. 2.8). Thus justification by faith undermines the arrogance of the clever, the powerful and the successful. And it does so, not by pretending that the cleverness, the power and the success do not exist. It does so by insisting that, real though they are, in the ultimate reckoning they count for nothing; for in the ultimate reckoning the only criterion is faith. It is the recognition, not merely in a form of words but at the deepest level of our being, that the fundamental character of life is that of gift. Both that we are and what we have it in us to become are not of our own contriving. They are grounded in the mysterious love of God from which the existence of the world and the particular historical tradition in which we stand derive. It is in the acceptance of that love, which for us is focused in the figure of Jesus, that our lives find their true meaning.

But I spoke of a second implication. God, says the Magnificat, puts down the mighty from their seat, but he also exalts the humble and meek. And justification by faith provides not only an answer to the sins of the mighty, the tendency to pride, to arrogance and to superiority; it provides also an answer to the needs of the weak. Indeed the two are often more closely interconnected than we realize. Those who appear outwardly to be proud and superior and aloof may well behave in such ways because at heart they are insecure, anxious and uncertain of themselves. If the sin of pride can be met by the recognition that we are justified by *faith* and by nothing else, the needs of the insecure can be met by the recognition that we are *justified* by faith. For behind that insecurity lurks so often fear – fear of failure, fear still more of what others will think of our supposed or real failures. We are afraid to give ourselves away; we are afraid of the judgments of others. And so we shut ourselves up within ourselves. But we do not have to be afraid of giving ourselves away, for we are not our own to give. We do not have to be afraid of the judgments of others, when the ultimate judgment has already been given in our favour. In Paul's language, 'it is God who justifies, who then can condemn?' (Rom. 8.33–4). This does not mean that the Christian will not have to face the anxieties, the failures and the misunderstandings that are the common lot of human life. Indeed he is liable to feel them the more acutely, as Jesus did, because the more convinced he is of the love of God, the more sensitive he becomes to the tragic element in life. But he is freed from the fear that these things may reach right through to and destroy the ultimate value and meaning of his life. For that is secure, secure by virtue of the graciousness of God. He is justified by faith.

The idiom of the gospel story and the idiom of Pauline theology are about as different from one another as they could be. Yet there is a congruence between the picture of Jesus and the picture of the person justified by faith. For at the heart of both lies an inner confidence, which is also a freedom from self-concern. It can be both, because it stems from an ultimate reference of all things to God as source and goal. We do not hesitate, as people once did, to say that Jesus lived by faith. To fail to do so is what seems odd to us. But I have gone a stage further, and sought to present him here as the prototype of the justified person. To conceive of Jesus as 'justified by faith' does still seem odd to us, because historically the phrase is so closely linked with the removal of sin and guilt. For Paul the inner confidence and freedom from self-concern of those who are justified is only possible because their sin and guilt have been dealt with by the blood of Christ's cross. However close the assimilation of the pictures of the Sonship of Jesus and the sonship to which the Christian is brought, at this point the parallel appears to break down absolutely. There is no direct analogy in the life of Jesus to that redemptive initiation by which the Christian receives his adoption as son. The Epistle to the Hebrews may speak of Jesus 'learning obedience through what he suffered', but the statement comes in a context where his sinlessness has just been affirmed (Heb. 5.8; 4.15); St Matthew recounts the baptism of Jesus by John, but is careful to make clear that in Jesus' case it is not a straightforward baptism of repentance (Matt. 3.13–17). In the sphere of redemption, therefore, Jesus is usually seen exclusively as agent and not as prototype. Yet redemption is a vital dimension of Christian experience, indispensable to any account of the way of faith.

Traditional doctrines of atonement are a source of deep dissatisfaction to almost all sensitive Christians. Their transactional character, whether expressed in terms of propitiation, substitution or payment of a debt, make them an easy butt for criticism. I have expressed my own unease about them in *The Remaking of Christian Doctrine*[8] and have no desire to add to those criticisms here. Yet the cross of Christ remains a powerful source of the experience of forgiveness and renewal. So it seems worthwhile to persevere with the approach to Jesus and the way of faith that I have been pursuing, and ask whether such an approach to the story of his death can better communicate those spiritual truths that atonement doctrine seeks to elucidate.

I want to come at the issue indirectly by way of reflection on what I regard as the two most important English works on the atonement in this century. In *Atonement and Personality*, R. C. Moberly was specifically aiming to get away from any conception of the atonement 'as *a transaction*, dramatically completed, and essentially outside ourselves'.[9] For him it is all important to insist that 'the sacrifice is to be, in its final consummation, the real transformation of us all'.[10] Yet his underlying attitude to scripture and tradition leads him to follow those words immediately with a qualification: 'But it is to be so in us because it was first the historical sacrifice, consecrated on Calvary, unique, all-sufficing; real between God and man in the Person of Jesus Christ, – and to each of us, as individuals, seen and believed in external objective history.'[11] Moberly's endeavour to speak of an all-sufficing sacrifice of an external objective historical kind, yet to do so in a fully personal way, led him to an interpretation of the passion and death of Jesus in terms of vicarious penitence.[12] In effect he was looking for an 'analogy in the life of Jesus to that redemptive initiation by which the Christian receives his adoption as son', something which I have declared to be absent. I do not believe that his interpretation will stand. The concepts of vicarious suffering and vicarious punishment are intelligible as concepts. There are other, primarily moral, objections to their use in the interpretation of Christ's death, but suffering and punishment are sufficiently external to a person that it makes sense to speak of someone undergoing them in his place. Moberly is to be applauded for his insistence that the mutual exclusiveness of human personalities can be exaggerated in falsely individual ways, yet the feeling of shame and sorrow at the sin of another to whom one is closely bound by nature and love, which he so eloquently describes, still falls short of constituting 'vicarious penitence' for that sin. In the last analysis the notion of vicarious penitence seems to me incapable of being given any meaning without recourse to interpretation of at least one of the two terms in an unreasonably Pickwickian sense.

But it is not only the ultimate failure of Moberly's bold and sensitive attempt to set out a doctrine of the atonement that would be true to tradition and to a personalist approach alike that is instructive. Instructive too is the response of two of his more informed and sympathetic critics. William Sanday insists against Moberly that 'the Scriptures do recognize a mysterious something which, in our imperfect human language, may be described as a "transaction". It seems to me difficult for the plain reader of the Bible to deny this.'[13] Moberly has only been able to avoid the idea of a transaction, and the concomitant notion of vicarious suffering, by means of a 'treatment of the Scriptural basis of the doctrine that is strangely unequal'.[14] In other words Moberly has, in Sanday's view, allowed his contemporary moral sensitivities to make him untrue to the biblical witness in a way which is illegitimate for 'those of us who start, not from any theological or philosophical system, but in the first instance from the Bible'.[15] The objection of Hastings Rashdall in a long review article in the *Journal of Theological Studies*,[16] on the other hand, is tilted in the opposite direction. As he sees it, it is a false view of the authority of scripture and of tradition that has held Moberly back from drawing out the full consequences of his deep and sensitive engagement with the moral and philosophical problems of atonement doctrine. He sums up his dissatisfaction with the book by declaring that 'whenever anything in the traditional view is shocking to the Reason and the moral consciousness, it is repudiated while formally under discussion, but assumed more or less undisguisedly in the subsequent argument'.[17] There is force in what both critics have to say. Any satisfactory synthesis of moral sensitivity and concern for scriptural witness of the kind that Moberly sought required a somewhat looser conception of the functioning of the authority of scripture than was generally held in the church at that time. But such a looser conception would come naturally today to many churchmen who would yet share the spirituality and generally conservative temper that characterizes Moberly's approach. It is important that we do not give up his search for a more personalist understanding of the meaning of the death of Jesus for the life of the Christian and of the church. It may be that the changed approach to scripture since Moberly's day opens up possibilities of interpretation for us that were not easily available to him.

The second book to which I want to refer, written more than fifty years later, is F. W. Dillistone's *The Christian Understanding of the Atonement*, which has received far less attention than it deserves. It draws widely not only on the varied traditional theories of atonement, but also on the wider resources of life and literature, of drama and music. It speaks of the various approaches it examines as 'analogues' or 'parables'. In other words, it emphasizes that theories of the atonement fulfil their role by way of appeal to the imagination; they indicate some experience of forgiveness or reconciliation within human relationships which may lift the imagination to grasp the fuller meaning of the cross.[18]

I find such an approach extremely congenial, for I too have been emphasizing throughout this book the analogical and parabolic character of all religious language. For Dillistone the parable lies in the characteristic human experiences that stand behind the various types of atonement theory. I am endeavouring here to approach the meaning of atonement more directly from the story of Jesus itself and of his death. For such an approach the category of parable is an appropriate one with which to begin. For Jesus' death was, as we have seen, an outcome of his ministry,[19] a ministry characterized by teaching in parables. It is sometimes suggested that that particular form of teaching was occasioned by the peculiar obduracy of his hearers; that indeed would seem to have been St Matthew's view.[20] At other times it has been suggested that the indirect parabolic approach was necessary because the salvific events of the gospel history – Jesus' own death and resurrection – had not yet taken place. But the fundamental reason is surely more basic still; it is simply that parable is the most appropriate form for the communication of God's word to mankind. Certainly the parables were no optional addendum to the message of Jesus, no mere form of sermon illustration. Many of them, as for example the parable of the wicked husbandmen (Mark 12.1–12), were at the centre of his conflict with the authorities. 'A direct line leads from the parables of Jesus to his crucifixion.'[21] Like poetic language in general, they served not only to disclose but to create reality, the reality of confrontation with the message of Jesus. Eta Linnemann gives forceful expression to this aspect of the parables:

> A successful parable is an event which decisively alters the situation. It creates a new possibility that did not exist before, the possibility that the man addressed can come to an understanding with the man addressing him across the opposition that exists between them. This possibility depends on the narrator bringing into language the matter which is in dispute between him and his listeners, and so opening up a new understanding.
>
> This new possibility which the parable creates in the situation is significant even if an understanding is not achieved. Even if the man addressed persists in his previous position, it is not simply 'all as before'. Just because a genuine opportunity has opened up for him of giving up his previous position, this has lost its inevitability. Even if he persists in it, he is really making a decision. His persistence acquires a different character; it becomes explicit opposition.
>
> So a successful parable is an event in a double sense; it creates a new possibility in the situation, and it compels the man addressed to a decision.[22]

Those words might have been written directly of the cross. To see the death of Jesus as the supreme example of parabolic speech about God is not to rob it of its objective character. It is still an event, creative of a new situation and calling for response.

If we speak of the cross as a parable, we excuse ourselves from being expected to provide a full explanation of its efficacy; but we do not excuse ourselves from giving some account of the direction in which its parabolic speech lifts the imagination and invites decision. For the basis of such an account I turn again to the ministry of Jesus, and to two features of it in particular that are most firmly rooted in the historical tradition.

If the characteristic words of Jesus in the gospel tradition are his parables, his characteristic actions are signs and miracles. For the critical reader today the miracle tradition is highly problematic. There can be little doubt that for the tradition to have arisen at all, Jesus must have been a remarkable exorcist and healer. Beyond that it is hard to speak with any confidence of the history that lies behind the tradition. But our concern is not simply with what happened, but with its meaning for those who developed and passed on the tradition. The healing ministry of Jesus is firmly set within the context of a conflict with evil. For Mark the healing miracles are particular engagements in a campaign of war against the demonic powers; for Luke they are signs of the coming of the kingdom, of the binding of the power of Satan (Luke 11.20–23). To say that for Jesus the world was aflame with the glory of God is not to ascribe to him the complacent belief that God's in his heaven and all's right with the world. He was committed to a struggle against all that disfigured God's world, so that the authentication of his ministry lay in what it was doing for the blind and the lame, the lepers and the deaf, the dead and the poor (Luke 7.22). But the way of the struggle was not the way of spectacular divine intervention. That way he had turned down in the temptation story, continued to reject in his refusal of every request for a sign and carried to its consummation in the face of the invitation to come down from the cross. So the cross is seen in continuity with the ministry as the culmination of a commitment to the conflict with evil which looks for no *deus ex machina* to solve its problems.

A similar picture emerges if we take as our starting-point that other characteristic action of Jesus, his association with publicans and sinners. For this, too, like the ministry of healing, was more than an act of compassion. The exclusion of those described as publicans and sinners from table fellowship was not just an act of churlishness. It was a conscientious action, in the interest of the attainment and preservation of holiness. So Jesus' action was a part of his challenge to the established

God's identification with men and women in their conflict with evil and depicts his succumbing to it rather than his denunciation of it. Does such a reading of the parable, it may be asked, do justice to the seriousness of sin? There are, of course, parables of judgment which have been used to give expression to God's condemnation of evil. They too can find their point of departure in the story of Jesus. For the recorded teaching of Jesus includes fierce denunciation of the Pharisees, as types of those who do not recognize the evil in themselves – fiercest of all in the saying about the unforgivable blasphemy against the Holy Spirit, where they appear as types of those who deliberately choose to call evil what is really and self-evidently good.[24] But such an approach cannot easily find a point of departure in the story of Jesus' death. As the story reaches its climax, the form of conflict involves condemnation only in a highly paradoxical sense. The reality and horror of evil are not played down there; indeed, they are more effectively displayed by the contrast with the integrity but accepting spirit of Jesus than they could have been by any form of spoken condemnation. Traditional Christian teaching has seldom taken the risk of dealing with evil in the way of Jesus. It has preferred to affirm the enormity of human sin in a more direct and unequivocal style.[25] '*Nondum considerasti quanti ponderis sit peccatum* – you have not yet considered how grave sin is.'[26] And in the light of that it has gone on to develop its parables of sin and judgment in so direct and non-parabolic a way, that it has even felt able to claim for the outcome of those developments what Anselm claims at the close of the *Cur Deus Homo* – that they 'would satisfy not only the Jews but also the pagans by reason alone'.[27] But such developments are not the criterion by which our way of seeing the story of Jesus' death is to be assessed. It would be nearer the truth to put it the other way round, that the story of Jesus' death is the criterion by which all such theological developments are to be assessed. But in reality the judgment that is called for needs to be more broadly based than either way of putting it allows.

5

The Church and the Purpose of God

I have attempted to interpret Christian sonship in the light of the Sonship of Jesus and in terms of the Pauline concept of justification, and have spoken of the way of faith as the working out of a personal decision in response to the new situation created by the cross. It might be objected that this presents Christian discipleship in unduly individualistic terms. That has sometimes been a fault in protestant emphasis on justification. But it need not be so; and rightly understood cannot be so. For to enter into sonship is automatically to enter into a special relationship with every other child of God. But how is 'every other child of God' to be understood? As we have seen earlier, the Christian tradition from its inception has seen identification with Christ as having implications with respect to both fellow-Christians in particular and fellow human beings in general.[1] The two desired implications have not always proved easy bedfellows. The former is the more dominant scriptural theme and it has also proved the more dominant motif historically.

Identification with Christ is most vividly depicted through the imagery of the body of Christ.[2] That image expresses in the most effective manner the indivisible character of the individual's union with Christ and with his or her fellow Christian. No one can be united to the head without also being united to the other limbs or members of the body. Individualistic Christianity is a contradiction in terms; the church is part of the gospel. But what of the Christian's relation to his fellow human being who does not share his Christian faith? The image of the body lends itself naturally to extension in terms of the outreach of Christ to those who do not acknowledge him. They are not, as yet at least, members of the body. They are to be treated with love, as Christ loved the world that did not receive him. But the primary implication of the image is that they are outside, they do not belong.

This suggestion of exclusiveness, of an emphasis on the difference between the Christian and the person who is not a Christian believer, is even more forcefully expressed by another basic image of the church: the church as the ark of salvation. Here the contrast is absolute. Those who are outside, are outside the only place of safety from the destruction that is the ultimate destiny of the surrounding, sinful world. Protestant sect and Catholic church alike have used this image and referred it to their own particular religious community. Thus Pius IX declared in 1854: 'It is to be held by faith that outside the apostolic Roman Church no one can be saved; it is the only ark of salvation and anyone who does not enter it will perish in the flood.'[3] The direct application of such language to a particular religious community, even the Roman Catholic Church, has to be repudiated as an intolerable narrowing of the divine purpose. Indeed, in an encyclical a century later the Roman Catholic Church explicitly abjured any such extreme interpretation of its language.[4]

But the fundamental difficulty in any such understanding of the church is not removed simply by extending the scope of its application in an ecumenical spirit. In his book, *Love's Endeavour, Love's Expense*, W. H. Vanstone has described how his own firm rejection of any such account grew out of a combination of pastoral experience and theological reflection. Called to establish a church life in a new housing development, he was forced to reflect on the purpose of the church's presence there. It was not needed, as it had been a generation earlier, to help ensure provision of the basic necessities of existence for the men and women of the district. How was its role to be understood? 'It might', he reflected, 'be the Ark in which a few, the faithful, are carried through death into the life to come.' The general difficulties inherent in such a claim were reinforced in his case by experiential knowledge of how chance rather than choice seemed to have been the determining factor in the presence of some within the church and the absence of others. 'It was repugnant to belief in a God of love and justice that chance-passengers in the Ark should be so richly rewarded, and those who, equally by chance, were absent so heavily penalised. If the new Church were God's instrument for selecting, identifying or preserving those who should be saved, then it was a crude and random instrument. To assert that God so intended or so used the Church would be to degrade and brutalise the concept of God.'[5] Indeed, any such use of the image of the ark is open to challenge, not only on the basis of the pastoral and theological arguments that Vanstone adduces, but also from within the scriptural story itself. For the climax of the story of the flood is the covenant of God with Noah, his descendants and every living creature that 'never again shall all flesh be cut off by the waters of a flood, and never again shall there be a flood to destroy the earth' (Gen. 9.9–11). If the flood is not to be the pattern of God's dealings with a still sinful world, the ark cannot be the pattern of his redemptive purpose. For flood and ark are correlatives that stand or fall together.

In practice the stark contrast between church and world which Vanstone denounces so vigorously would find comparatively little support among Christians today. Many may even be surprised that he felt the need to entertain the idea and argue with it so explicitly at all. Other writers speak as if such an idea was a matter simply of past history. 'The visible Church is no longer regarded as the community of the exclusively saved,' writes Charles Davis;[6] and Karl Rahner avers that 'the fact that the history of salvation is coexistent with the history of the whole world . . . no longer poses any special problem today for the normal interpretation of Christianity.'[7] Yet however much we may repudiate it at the conscious level, the power of the image still remains. Can we speak, and still more importantly can we feel, positively about the church without this element of a contrast of eternal significance between church and world, which the image of the ark so forcefully conveys and which other images of the church also carry, even if somewhat less sharply? Is our vision of the church something more than a milk-and-water version of the one we can no longer stomach? Or can we draw constructively on the climax of the flood story, the Noachic covenant between God and every living creature of all flesh in the direction that Karl Rahner's bold affirmation suggests?

If we are to do so, we must go back to more basic reflection about God's purpose for the world. The story of mankind is the story of the gradual emergence of self-conscious human persons. This can be presented as a process of increasing individuation over against the collective existence of herd or tribe. But such a presentation can easily mislead. To be a person is not the same as to be a self-sufficient individual. The richness of personal existence is dependent on continuing relations with other people. The emergence of persons involves not the removal of the communal but its transformation. It is in the light of this basic characteristic of human nature that the vital importance of the church in Christian faith is primarily to be seen. In the words of Karl Rahner, 'We are aware today in a quite new and inescapable way that man is a social being, a being who can exist only within such intercommunication with others throughout all of the dimensions of human existence. And from this perspective we acquire a new understanding of Christian religion as an ecclesial religion.'[8]

All this is reflected in the records of the Old Testament. In some of its earlier stories the people of Israel are depicted as a society, the interrelation of whose members is less than fully personal. The members of Achan's family are so closely identified with him that they have to suffer with him for his sin (Josh. 7.16–25). They are not seen as full persons in their own right. The later vision of Jeremiah's new covenant gives a new status to each individual member of the people of God. But it is not a charter of individualism. It is still a covenant between God and his people, but it is to be a covenant with a people where 'no longer shall each man teach his neighbour and each his brother saying "Know the Lord", for they shall all know me, from the least of them to the greatest, says the Lord' (Jer. 31.34). The vision is of a community in which personal life is not restricted but brought to its fullest expression.

No community measures up to that ideal. There are two principal ways in which communities fall short of it. Though necessary to personal flourishing, no community is ever perfectly adapted to that purpose; all societies inhibit as well as enhance personal life. There are depersonalizing aspects of the functioning of nation states, even when they avoid the more obvious forms of tyranny. Smaller groupings, like families, seldom escape exercising a narrowing or restrictive influence, even if they avoid those more subtle forms of tyranny of which they can be guilty. Moreover, all societies are limited in scope and derive some of their communal strength from standing over against other groups who are seen as the common enemy. Communal strife and even wars are intimately bound up with that experience of belonging to one's own group which contributes so profoundly to the meaning and purpose of personal life. People still look back nostalgically to the spirit that characterized Britain in the days of the blitz.

The church saw itself as a fulfilment of the prophecy of Jeremiah. Whether or not Jesus spoke of a new covenant at the last supper with Jeremiah's words in mind,[9] the link is explicit in the Epistle to the Hebrews (10.16–17). Integral to its message is the hope of removing the two shortcomings that are characteristic of human societies – the narrowing impact of the collective on the personal and the lack of a universal dimension. Because Christianity emerges out of Judaism, the promise of the church is set over against what are seen as the particular failings of Judaism. Christian freedom is contrasted with the restrictiveness of the law, and the universal invitation of the gospel with the national character of Jewish faith. These contrasts are to be found both in the gospel traditions about Jesus and in the argumentation of the Pauline epistles. Jesus challenges the way in which the law operates in society as one that 'loads men with burdens hard to bear' (Luke 11.46); and that is the obverse of its true purpose, for 'the sabbath was made for man, not man for the sabbath' (Mark 2.27). That is not to say that the way of the disciple is easy. It is a way of self-denial, of taking up the cross, even of losing one's life; yet it is the way of life (Mark 8.34–5). So, too, for Paul the law is a form of slavery; the gospel opens the way to freedom, to the sonship that is man's birthright (Gal. 3.23–4.7; 5.1). Similarly, both the creative bounty of God's sun and rain and the redemptive goal of the prophetic ministry adumbrated in the Old Testament know no barriers of race or nation (Matt. 5.45; Luke 4.25–7). The Christian churches that were the fruit of Paul's preaching were to be open to Jew and Gentile alike (Gal. 3.28). How far the negative aspects implicit in these early Christian claims to freedom and universality represent fair criticisms of the Judaism of Paul's day is an important and much disputed historical question.[10] What is important here is not the degree of their historical justification, but the form of the hope held out for the new Christian community. The claim was that the power of the Holy Spirit, made available in a new way by the ministry, death and resurrection of Jesus, was establishing a community of which freedom and universality would be the hallmarks. Enough of what was hoped for was experienced in those early Christian communities to give them that inner vitality and attractiveness which won the allegiance of so many in the Graeco-Roman world. But the problems inherent in the existence of communities did not disappear. Whatever the justice of the Christian charges against first-century Judaism, the same charges have needed to be levelled against the church throughout its history. The scriptural importance of the critique of Pharisaism is not its historical reliability but its existential application to the Christian church.

But the hope remains important, the hope that in the church the Spirit of God is establishing a community of which freedom and universality are to be the hallmarks. The church is a contributory agent in the divine purpose for mankind, in which repressive collective is to be transformed into true community and true community learn to find a source of communal life that is not dependent on hostility to other communities. There is much in the teaching of Jesus and in the record of the church's history that might seem to support the view that the institutional life of the church stands in inevitable and direct conflict with such a goal. 'Christ,' wrote Simone Weil in her notebooks, 'expressly forbade his followers to seek authority and power. Therefore his Congregation (the Church) ought not to be a society.'[11] But that represents an unbalanced interpretation of the evidence. For all its dangers, the institution is not to be seen in purely negative terms. 'The Church as institution can preserve as well as corrupt the Church as community; it can express and define through word and deed the common mind as well as thwart the common spirit.'[12] A similar ambivalence arises from reflection on the studies of sociologists. For while they serve to show the important role played by institutions as such, their accounts of how communities operate do not offer much encouragement to the Christian's hope for the church. But it is not as the source of his or her hopes that the Christian turns to the work of the sociologists; for their observations are of what has been observed to happen, not of what may happen. What the Christian seeks to gain from their descriptions of the way communities function is a more realistic appraisal of what particular steps to be taken now may best contribute to the pursuit of the church's goal.

It is important, therefore, to try to understand what it is within the life of the church that has impeded the realization of its hopes and made it so often similar in character to the Judaism which at its inception it saw as the antithesis of its true self. All communities need rules or laws. Laws are not necessarily restrictive of true freedom; rather they provide the form or structure that is necessary to the development of personal life. But if they are to fulfil that role, they must be open to change and modification in the face of changing circumstances. Too rapid change gives rise to destructive anarchy; failure to change results in alienating rigidity. The Christian who recognizes the constructive contribution of structure and rules sees them not as unfortunate necessities, but as the gift of God. He seeks to give them a positive theological evaluation. The motives behind the attempt are right; but its execution has tended to make an already difficult task more difficult.

Nowhere is this more evident than in the case of the church's understanding of its own ministry. Like any other society, it needs authorized officials for the better ordering of its common life. The emergence of a fixed pattern of ministry in the church is a complex story. Pragmatic considerations played an important part in it. Ignatius' advocacy of episcopal authority, an important court of appeal for later catholic tradition, is closely linked to the practical needs of the small, threatened communities of Asia Minor to which he writes.[13] But for the Christian, practical arrangements that make for the good ordering of society, and thereby for the deepening of personal life, are contributions to the divine purpose for the world; they are vehicles of the grace of God. So from the outset the ministry was seen and interpreted in theological terms. The bishop is a symbol of the unity of God, the presbyters of the apostles and the deacons of the servant-ministry of Jesus.[14] To this symbolic understanding of the ministry, subsequent generations (starting

later in the second century) added a further theological interpretation in terms of a continuous historical chain of episcopal
ministry going back to the direct appointment of Jesus himself.[15]
Such theological interpretations can serve the valuable purpose
of helping the community at large to see the ministry, not just
as more or less competent human practitioners but as mediators
of the grace of God. But in practice they have done more than
that, and the more has often proved destructive of their proper
goal. Christian faith speaks of God's eternal changelessness. It
was an emphasis particularly characteristic of the early centuries of the church's life. To see something as a symbol of God
himself or as expressive of his will and intention naturally suggests that that something also should be maintained unchanged.
The particular interpretations themselves do not necessarily
carry so absolute an implication. The symbolism in terms of
God, the apostles and Jesus Christ clearly cannot be regarded as
a coherent symbolic interpretation of the threefold ministry as
a single whole; nor does it exclude other symbolic understand-
ings of other patterns of ministry. Furthermore, the actual
history of the development of the ministry does not point to so
direct an authorization of later episcopal ministry as the traditional theologically motivated story suggests. What has under-
lain the strongly held insistence on the absolute necessity of an
episcopal or threefold ministry has been the deep-seated feeling
that if the ministry is to have a theological grounding at all,
then that pattern of ministry must be the eternal will of God for
all time and all places. In seeing the law as God's gracious will
for his people, Judaism was led to speak of it as eternal, coexistent with God before the creation of the world. It was a
noble conception, but carried with it the risk of being taken too
literally and thereby leading to too fixed an understanding of the
operation of the law, with all the attendant dangers of legalism.
The same principle has been at work in the church's understanding of her ministry with the same attendant dangers.[16]

Those dangers can be illustrated in three ways. A pattern of ministry that enhances personal life within the community in one set of social conditions, may come to have the opposite effect in another. The Christian ministry developed in an age with a comparatively fixed, hierarchical conception of the structure of human society. The shape of the church's ministry reflected that of the ordering of the society within which it was set. The advantages and disadvantages of that development can be variously evaluated, but it is clear that there were important advantages. It was not only a natural way of ordering the life of the church, but helped people to make Christian sense of their life within society. But that pattern of society has been drastically altered by the intellectual and technological changes of the second millennium of the Christian era. Meanwhile, for many Christians the hierarchical structure of the Christian ministry, seen as an eternal God-given reality, has remained unchanged in essence. Some would claim that thereby it gives much needed security in a perplexing world of flux; but to others it seems now (whatever may have been true in earlier ages) to be inappropriate for an era of great social mobility. To Charles Davis its tendency to make for repression in the changed circumstances of today's world was a major reason for leaving the Roman Catholic Church.[17]

Even where the fixity of ministry does not give rise to the kind of oppressiveness of which Charles Davis speaks, there is still a risk that it may receive disproportionate attention in the church's reflection on its own way of life. Such lack of a sense of proportion is no small danger in the spiritual life. It is an important feature in the critique of Pharisaism in the gospels (e.g. Luke 11.42), which as we have seen is of primary concern to Christians for what it says to the Christian church. The furtherance of personal life which lies at the heart of the church's concern does not lend itself to treatment with the same degree of precision as orders of ministry. The forms of personal life are infinitely varied. Any general principles appropriate to this sphere are best expressed in the more indirect style of parable and story. These need to be supplemented by continuing study of the ever changing conditions in which people's lives are set in order to grasp what their proper application involves at any particular time. But that is a hard and elusive task. We feel more at home, more secure with what is fixed. So issues where greater precision seems possible tend to prove more attractive and loom larger in the life of the church than their relative importance warrants. In a sermon preached at the enthronement of Bishop Westcott, F. J. A. Hort drew attention to this danger by speaking of how 'the essential realities of life and service between the members of a church one with another, or of each with the whole, have been obscured by the greater permanence and definiteness of what we are accustomed to call its organisation'.[18] Few would be bold enough to claim that we have progressed very far in redressing such disproportion since Hort's day.

But the point at which the dangers of which I have been speaking are most evident in the life of the contemporary church are the restrictions that they are allowed to exercise on the relations between Christians of differing denominations. Too few Christians are prepared to acknowledge that forms of ministry which have been and are a means of grace to them, bearing an appropriate theological interpretation within their community, might yet need to be modified or to stand equally side by side with other forms of ministry. Any such suggestion is seen as a challenge to their religious role or theological propriety. But it is a challenge only to their religious or theological completeness, a challenge which any Christian ought to welcome rather than resist. To speak in such terms is not to deny that there are real problems and differences of substance to be worked through in the drawing together of the churches. But it is to claim that the concentration on different forms of ministry as a major barrier in such drawing together is the result of a fundamental misjudgment in the church's theological understanding of itself and of its ministry.

'The law which promised life proved to be death to me',

wrote Paul (Rom. 7.10). In his struggle to relate the liberating character of his Christian experience to his Jewish religious heritage, Paul found himself forced into making the paradoxical affirmation that the God-given law, which he still had to acknowledge to be 'holy and just and good' (Rom. 7.12), had become for him an obstacle to the working of God's grace. The church needs to acknowledge a similarly bitter irony in its own life. The structures of its institutional life, which are necessary to it and rightly spoken of as God's gift to the church, have frequently proved themselves a barrier to the fulfilment of its true role. And this has happened not because they have been regarded too lightly or their God-given character ignored, but precisely because they have been taken too theologically – or more accurately because they have been taken theologically in the wrong way. So to challenge any understanding of the church which speaks in terms of the permanence of its structures and of its ministry in particular, is not to offer a lower or reductionist account of them. It is rather an attempt to recall the church, and our theological understanding of it, to its true function in the economy of God.

I spoke earlier of two characteristics of human societies, which the church gives promise of overcoming. It is to be seen not only as the society that should promote most fully the personal life of its members, but also as one that does not need to derive its communal sense from opposition to other groups. If the true source of its common life is the unifying power of the Spirit of Christ, it ought not to have the same need of such external stimuli as other groups do. Yet the history, particularly but not exclusively, of the smaller Christian sects gives the lie to such expectations. They are classic examples of groups whose corporate sense is largely provided by their alienation from the rest of society. Yet the purpose of the church, as we have been trying to understand it, is to contribute to the growth of the unity of all God's creation (cf. Eph. 1.10). And for the most part the church has tried to hold on to that wider commitment.

Even from within the context of seeing the church as the one ark of salvation, a duty of universal evangelization has generally been maintained. But the universality of the church has also been declared in more comprehensive terms than simply that of having a message of universal application. To quote again from Hort's sermon, 'the rightful province of the church can be no narrower than the entire world of humanity, because God in Christ has claimed all things human except the evil that corrupts them'.[19] But what does such grand language mean? Can the 'entire world of humanity' be 'the rightful province of the church' in any meaningful sense beyond that of the church's readiness to undertake practical service and evangelization on a world-wide scale?

We are back with the problem that faced Bill Vanstone setting out to establish the life of the church on a new housing estate. Is there an understanding of the church which is true to the empirical reality of the church and at the same time does justice to the loving majesty of God? And if there is, can the church articulate its universal role in broader terms than those of a universal message to all who stand outside its boundaries, without running the risk of emasculating its gospel? Vanstone's answer to his own problem is grounded in his vision of God as the 'God who will not abandon and to Whom nothing, save Himself, is expendable'.[20] For that implies that the loving creativity of God is at work in the world no more and no less than it is at work in the church. What is distinctive about the church is not that it is uniquely or differentially the locus of the divine activity; rather it is the place where the loving activity of God is recognized and acknowledged. 'The meaning of the Church is that in its being creative love achieves the triumphant completion of its work in being recognized as love. Therefore upon the being or non-being of the Church depends the final triumph or tragedy of love – the triumph of being known as love, the tragedy of remaining unknown.'[21] Karl Rahner similarly sees the supernatural grace of God as universal in its operation, and therefore 'the church is not the society of those who alone are saved, but the sign of the salvation of those who, as far as its historical and social structure is concerned, do not belong to it'.[22]

What is important about these statements is that they combine a vigorous repudiation of the exclusive approach to salvation with a strong positive affirmation about the church. It is the place where love is recognized as love, and thereby contributes to, even constitutes, the triumph of love. This is in line with our earlier claim that the imaginative construction whereby certain occurrences in human history are seen as acts of God is a step of great significance in the furtherance of the divine purpose.[23] But what is of paramount importance is that the love that it recognizes is not a love that is directed to itself in an exclusive or privileged way. The love that it recognizes is the universal love of God, whether that be expressed by Vanstone in terms of God's creative love or by Rahner in terms of supernatural grace. It is that fact which provides the potential for the church's fulfilment of its universal role. For that which gives it its distinctiveness as a particular, limited society is something which does not set it against other groups, but which in important respects unites it with them as they now are and so frees it from the temptation to see them only as recruiting grounds for further members of its own society.

Yet inherent in such a universal role is a tension which is not easily resolved even in theory, let alone in practice. The repudiation of an exclusivist view of salvation does not involve the repudiation of a missionary dimension. Its task may be seen differently; it will not, in Rahner's terms, be so much a matter of 'turning "non-Christians" into something they are not as trying to bring them to their true selves'. But the Christian will still 'go out into the world with missionary zeal and bear witness in the name of Christ. He will wish to give of his grace to others, for the explicit self-awareness of grace in the Church, is itself a grace'.[24] And coexisting with this continuing, if revised, missionary concern is the task of contributing to the wider human community, where the love of God remains unrecognized. This is the aspect of the church's task most strongly emphasized by Charles Davis. Christian fellowship is for him 'not the establishment of an exclusive Christian fellowship' but 'the discovery and building up of universal human fellowship.' 'The visible Church,' he says, 'reaches out to the total human reality and merges into the universal human community.'[25] So the church needs to preserve, to develop and to share its distinctive recognition of God's love in Christ, but at the same time to value and to foster the growth of that wider human fellowship, to whose vital significance both the New Testament and the contemporary human situation bear eloquent testimony. It is something it will never perfectly achieve. But it is to be seen as a dual principle by which the *ecclesia semper reformanda* must seek always to reform itself. And if it is to do that, it will need, like the individual Christian, to learn from its Lord the principle of life through death. John Drury has put the point provocatively in terms of the individual Christian: 'A person is rescued from the self-centred solipsism of worrying "am I a Christian?" by the gospel which says he must lose his life . . . for God and neighbour if he would really find it. To put it very sharply, it is only the Christian who does not much care whether he is one who is one: necessarily so if love of God and neighbour is what it is all about.'[26] If that is the principle whereby the individual Christian is taken out of himself and enabled to be united with his neighbour in a distinctively Christian way, may not the same principle apply to the life of the church? To put it very sharply, it is only the church which does not much care whether it is one which is one. By that standard churches are hard to come by.

6

Worship and Action

Most doctrines of the church have a ring of unreality about them – and mine is certainly no exception. It is not necessarily a fault, for any such doctrine must deal with the church as it is, yet not only as it is but also as it is intended to be in the purposes of God. One early Christian writer combines this dual aim in a single image when he depicts the church as an old woman, image alike of its eternal existence in the presence of God and of its contemporary weakness in the quality of the lives of its members.[1] But if an element of unreality cannot be wholly eliminated, it certainly lays an obligation on us to attempt further, if indirect, ways of clarification. I have emphasized two features as fundamental to the being of the church. It is the place where the love of God is recognized and consciously acknowledged with a response of gratitude and love; and it is a society intended to contribute to that divine purpose of love by the furtherance of personal life not only among its members but universally. So we can best penetrate more deeply into the nature of the church by consideration of its worship and of its moral teaching.

At the heart of the church's life, then, is the acknowledgment in love and gratitude of the love of God. So the central act of Christian worship is called 'eucharist' or thanksgiving. In mediaeval and Reformation rites that thanksgiving is concentrated on the cross; but while that has always been the focus, some of the earliest recorded liturgies show a much wider range of thanksgiving, incorporating the whole story of God's creation and of his dealings with his people. This fuller range of thanksgiving is a characteristic also of more recently revised or constructed rites.[2]

But why such emphasis on thanksgiving and adoration? Even those who conceive the ultimate source of life in ways that are less than personal sometimes experience life as something good that they have received, but there is no one to whom they can meaningfully offer any expression of gratitude or adoration. Those on the other hand who conceive God in the most directly personal, and thereby anthropomorphic, way have a natural outlet for their feelings of thanksgiving. Yet there seems something odd about God's apparent desire for continual praise. The oddity finds lively expression from the pen of the great liturgical scholar, E. C. Ratcliff.

> 'The only way we can cleanse our spirits is by praising the things that deserve praise. That's why the theologians say it is a duty to praise God – not for the Almighty Sultan's sake, but for our own.' Herein are seen the value and the necessity of worship, both for our life as individuals, and also for the corporate life of the local Christian community . . . But for worship to be catharsis, it must be true adoration – i.e., concentration upon God, exclusive of thoughts about ourselves.[3]

The implicit paradox has close parallels in other aspects of human experience. The deepest joys of love and friendship are only to be found when a person stops actively seeking them and forgets himself in the concentration of his affection on the person of the beloved or the friend. For worship to be worship it must be wholly unself-regarding, the concentration of every faculty on that which is of ultimate worth, namely God himself. Yet it is *we* who are worshipping; it is *our* spirits that are to be cleansed; it is *we*, not God, who are bettered by it. So though the act of worship itself must be self-forgetful, its forms require to be determined with regard to the needs and characters of the worshippers. In any event we have no means of making the forms of our worship true to God as he is in himself, as distinct from our limited apprehensions of him. So any critical reflection on the nature and the forms of worship must be carried out in close relation to the kind of general reflection on Christian faith on which we are engaged.

In the light of the argument so far, there are three principles that need to be borne in mind. (1) The language of faith is an imaginative construction, reaching out towards a mystery at the limits of human experience (Ch. 2). The *vox orandi* must be true to its imaginative, evocative role. (2) For the Christian, the particular shape of his or her response to the mystery is a sonship made effective by the Sonship of Jesus, and pre-eminently by the historical parable of his death and resurrection (Ch. 4). These must therefore be the factors that shape the Christian's worship also. (3) Christian life involves membership of a continuing community, designed to further God's purpose of a world-wide human fellowship (Ch. 5). The church's worship therefore must be true to this wider vision, and not just to the evident needs of its individual members here and now. We shall therefore make these three issues the starting-point of our reflections.

1. If the *vox orandi* is to be evocative of the mystery of God, where is such a voice to be heard? I have spoken earlier of its kinship with the voice of the poet. But worship is a corporate activity, and the voice of most poets is too esoteric in character. Few poets, especially today, speak to as wide a range of their contemporaries as the language of worship is required to do. The primary source for the evocative language of worship cannot be found in the present; it is given in images that have established themselves over a long period of time and have come to fulfil a symbolic role within the life of the worshipping community.[4] So worship has, and must have, a strongly traditional and conservative character about it.

That is a vital consideration; but it is not the only consideration, as some of the oversimplified polemic against contemporary liturgical revision would appear to suggest. 'Old words are one of the best devices for aiding the sense of mystery,' writes Leslie Houlden.[5] But he also recognizes the danger that the older images and concepts may have lost the roots they once had in human lives. They may have become 'so far removed from readily accessible imagery that [their] evocative power is minimal, except for the initiated'.[6] This is not to ask for instant worship that makes no demand on the worshipper. It is to recognize the danger that an exclusively traditionalist approach can give rise to an esotericism as serious as would be the esotericism of worship based on the imagery of a difficult contemporary poet. And it is the traditionalist danger that is both more common and more subtle. For it is *we* who are to be attuned to the mystery of God. And if the imagery through which that is being done is imagery that is unrelated to our daily lives, then worship is likely to become an escapist rather than a transforming influence in life.

The bringing together of the sense of the other and of the everyday is integral to worship, but there is a tension between the two that no ordering of worship will ever fully resolve. In the act of worship itself, it is the self-forgetful evocation of the other that is primary. But for all its self-forgetfulness it is an essential aim of the act of worship that the worshipper receive inspiration and transformation, not just at a conscious surface level but at the deeper levels of his being. And for that to be achieved, however long-standing the imagery that is used may need to be, it must not be archaic; it must be imagery that is not wholly removed from the ways in which we see and interpret our everyday lives.

2. Evocation of a sense of mystery is not the sole aim of worship. For the Christian, the sense of God has received specific articulation in terms of the fatherhood of God.[7] The symbol of fatherhood does not simply remove the sense of mystery, but

it incorporates within it that sense of confidence which we have earlier discussed in terms of the Sonship of Jesus and the Pauline doctrine of justification.[8] This combination of hiddenness and nearness, of awe and intimacy in the Christian apprehension of God, needs to find appropriate embodiment in the forms of Christian worship. The interweaving of the two motifs calls for subtle and allusive expression. There is a further tension here that will never be wholly removed. Different occasions and different aspects of worship call for different emphases. It is appropriate that the Lord's Prayer should sometimes be introduced by the lesser litany ('Lord have mercy upon us, Christ have mercy upon us, Lord have mercy upon us') and sometimes by the words 'We are bold to say . . .' There is a significant difference in the mood evoked by the different introductions. Both have a proper place in Christian worship.

But the Sonship of Jesus does not only characterize Christian worship by giving to it a sense of confidence that would otherwise be lacking in man's address to the ultimate mystery of God. The recognition that anxiety is not integral to awe is certainly an important feature of Christian spirituality. But the tradition of christocentric worship is far more explicit than that. And it is this explicitly christocentric character of worship that seems to many people the major stumbling-block against accepting the kind of account that I have offered of the person of Jesus as one that can properly claim to stand within the continuity of lived Christian faith.

The basic form of this christological liturgical tradition is the offering of all prayer to God 'through Jesus Christ our Lord'. We are so familiar with it that we tend to forget how oddly it consorts with traditional trinitarian teaching. The underlying image is of approach to an imperial sovereign, made possible by the agency of an intermediary, of a friend at court. But the imagery is doubly unsuitable to Christian faith. In the first place it suggests an understanding of God that is from a Christian point of view seriously out of balance. But still further, it cannot stand without the implication of divisions within the Trinity or between the humanity and divinity of Christ of a kind wholly unacceptable to orthodox belief. So the underlying imagery has been allowed happily to fall away. Separated from their imaginative origins, the words run the risk of becoming no more than a formula, a badge of belonging with no specific meaning of their own. That need not be their fate. For the words can be, and are, taken to mean that we are enabled to approach God as we do on the basis of what he has done for us and what we have come to know of him through Jesus Christ. Such an understanding of worship is fully consonant with, indeed is required by, the understanding of the significance of Jesus for faith that I have outlined earlier.

But worship is not offered only *through* Jesus Christ, it may be offered *to* him also. The origins of this practice belong partly to an early tradition of popular piety and partly to later developments consciously motivated by a desire to reinforce newly established theological orthodoxy.[9] It is characteristic of hymnody rather than of the more austere form of collect prayer. It is a practice that cannot be accepted simply at its face value by any form of theological tradition. The Trinitarian cannot allow that prayer is ever offered to Christ to the exclusion of the other persons of the Trinity. For God is one and is the only proper object of all Christian prayer or worship. The difference between praying to Christ and praying to God the Father is not easily spelt out. 'Prayer to Christ,' writes Geoffrey Lampe, 'seems to be so completely identical with prayer to God who was revealed in Christ that nothing is lost if the "Christ" to whom it is addressed is translated into "God who was in Christ".'[10] Indeed, at the level of formal theological reflection not only is nothing lost, but much is gained. Yet the address of some prayers exclusively to Christ may be allowed because the theme on which the prayer concentrates is one that is particularly linked in our minds with some aspect of God's self-revelation in Jesus. Its justification lies in its evocative power

96

for us. It must not be treated as direct description of the ultimate destiny of the prayer being offered. I have stressed earlier the importance of concrete imagery in the language of faith, and the bold forms of direct predication to which it can rightly give rise.[11] So for one whose faith in God finds its shape through the records of Jesus, the direct address to Christ in the poetic form of hymnody or in the context of more informal occasions of prayer will not seem inappropriate. It is part of that direct use of imagery that is essential to the flourishing of faith. Once the poetic and evocative style that is essential to the language of faith is recognized, I do not believe that the christological character of traditional Christian worship is incompatible with the understanding of the figure of Jesus that I have outlined here and in other writings. Much of it is a splendid embodiment of the significance of Jesus for faith, cast as it should be in the *vox orandi* rather than the *vox credendi*.

But there is another way in which the christological tradition of worship, valuable though it is, may have a distorting effect, not this time with regard to the conception of the Godhead addressed in prayer but with regard to the range of human experience on which the act of worship is seen to draw. The primary association of the eucharist is with the last supper of Jesus with his disciples, the death on the cross which it foreshadowed and the resurrection that followed. This remains true whether or not Jesus himself consciously inaugurated the rite.[12] It is proper that it should be so, for that complex of events is for the Christian the supreme parable of the love of God. They are the events which provide the basic articulation of the Christian's apprehension of God. But eucharistic thanksgiving is not restricted to those redemptive events; its range, as we have seen, is far wider.[13] So too the symbolism of bread and wine is not something exclusive to the Christian tradition, nor something that emerged wholly new from the action of Jesus like Athene from the head of Zeus. In debates about the origins of the Christian sacraments, some scholars have argued against any influence of the mystery religions, as if the admission of any such influence might contaminate the religious purity of the eucharistic rite. But such fears are unwarranted. The broad base of eucharistic symbolism is an enrichment, not a watering down of its religious significance.[14] The historical foundations of the eucharist in the ministry of Jesus and its immediate aftermath do not need to be played down. Christ puts his transforming stamp on every aspect of those human rituals and experiences which have contributed to its growth in human history, but he does not swamp them. Grace does not abolish nature, but perfects it.

The tradition of Christian worship is a many-splendoured thing, a source of grace to an infinite variety of men and women. To say that is not to claim that it is free from blemish, that all is for the best in the best of all possible churches. Every Christian will find within it particular causes of offence and even of dismay. Some of the sources Christians use go back before the time of Christ and, like certain features of the Psalms, embody a spirit alien to his. The same is true of explicitly Christian sources too, for the makers of liturgy were fallible human beings like ourselves. Thus John Burnaby speaks of 'prayers like the Collect for the Fourth Sunday in Lent, and still more the sentences, as terrible in meaning as they are grand in diction, which for innumerable mourners have accompanied the committal of a beloved body to the grave' as 'striking tones not easily recognizable as those of the Spirit of God's Son'.[15] In any case, the dynamic character of human existence makes it inevitable that many a hymn or prayer will embody a theology or speak an idiom that few Christians today can conscientiously adopt as a natural expression of their own beliefs. That must be accepted as a necessary concomitant of the irreplaceable role played by ancient tradition in the evocative function of worship. And once we do accept that, the way is open to enjoy that tradition as a whole, free from scrupulosity, as a powerful though imperfect medium of the grace of God.

3. If all is not for the best in the best of all possible churches, it is equally certain that all is not for the best in the best of all possible worlds. Christian faith does not only affirm the mystery of God and the greatness of the redemption achieved in Jesus. It speaks also of a future hope, of a work yet to be brought to fulfilment in God's transformation of the world. So Christian worship is concerned not only with the evocation of wonder and of response to what has been received through Christ, but with the future coming of God's kingdom. It is concerned not only to see God in and through what is, but to contribute to the determination of what shall be. In the context of worship this concern about the future takes the form of petition and intercession, prayers that certain things may happen for the person praying or for others.

The conviction that the right approach to God or the gods can effect what will happen to the suppliant is a feature of almost all forms of religion. In its crudest form the belief is held that if the correct form of address is used, the desired outcome cannot fail. The belief that the right prayer is effective automatically may be regarded as the distinguishing mark between magic and religion. But the distinction is not always easy to draw. For even when the outcome is not thought to be automatic, failure to receive the answer desired is frequently ascribed to some defect in the praying. Belief in the direct efficacy of true prayer to change what would otherwise have happened in the world is a common feature not only of popular Christianity, but of other religions too. I cite one example from a letter, in the correspondence columns of a Nichiren Buddhist journal, written to illustrate 'the power of chanting'.[16] The author describes his action on returning home to find a fire raging fiercely and out of control in his street.

> I rushed into my house with my brother . . . we knelt down and chanted daimoku. We chanted for our house to be saved, otherwise we would be left homeless. Despite the inferno

which was just a few feet away, we kept on chanting . . . the fire began to go out just about two feet away from my house. The firemen and the crowd who witnessed it could hardly believe it.

It would be easy to produce comparable stories from Christian sources. It is easy too to pour scorn on them as really falling on the magic side of the divide between magic and religion. Yet the gospels are full of sayings that seem to support such a view. 'Ask and it shall be given you' (Matt. 7.7); 'Whatever you ask in prayer, believe that you receive it, and you will' (Mark 11.24). And there are thoughtful theologians and philosophers prepared to insist that 'petition is the heart of prayer',[17] and that petition does involve asking God to produce effects in the natural world.

Yet it is precisely this understanding of petition and the conception of divine action that it involves which are so problematic for many Christians today.[18] I have already argued that the concept of divine action needs to be understood in terms of final rather than of efficient causation.[19] Is such an understanding compatible with the church's practice of petition and intercession? At the heart of the Lord's Prayer, which is at the heart of the prayers of the church, stand the words 'Thy kingdom come; thy will be done'. They involve both petition and intercession, since the place where God's will is to be done is not only the person praying but others also. How are these prayers to be understood? In a valuable discussion, John Burnaby summarizes the underlying assumptions with which the problem needs to be approached in these words:

The Christian faith implies . . . (a) that the kingdom of God is to be promoted in human history by no other power than the power of love, and (b) that the power of God's love takes effect in human history in no other way than through the actions and wills of men in whom that love has come to dwell.[20]

that his initial approach might seem destined to result in our 'confining our prayers to the request for our own growth in charity in the terms of the Collect for Quinquagesima'.[26] He is naturally and rightly resistant to what would be so solipsistic a style of Christian prayer. Indeed there would be an element of self-contradiction for the church's prayer to be so narrowly circumscribed, when at the heart of the purpose of the church is its contributing to the divine purpose for world-wide human fellowship. But how is this wider range of intercessory prayer to be understood? It can only be, we have argued, in ways consistent with the promotion of the kingdom of God by the power of love alone and its taking effect in history through the actions and wills of men and women. How human wills are moved to love what is truly worth loving is something we do not fully understand. So the way is open for Burnaby to speak of the union of our wills with God's in prayer as a means by which 'the universal working of the love of God has increase' in ways 'we must be content not to know'.[27] Peter Baelz writes in similar vein: 'We may give the divine love a *point d'appui* so that through our prayer it may realize possibilities which only in this way it can actualize. Perhaps we must go on praying in the faith and hope that this is so, even though we cannot yet explain how it is so.'[28] Such acknowledgments of the limitation of our knowledge in this sphere are healthy. But we do not need to postulate some hidden form of instrumental causation to justify our intercessory practice. For myself I am content to say that if in praying I am to spread out the desires of my heart before God, they cannot but include concern for the well-being of others; indeed any progress in Christian life must surely extend the degree to which that is so. Here I kneel, I can do no other. Many of the old forms of prayer do not ideally express what I am doing, for I do not envisage my prayers as having any direct causative effect on those for whom I pray. But something that stands in continuity with those older forms of intercession seems to me a necessary part of the building up of a community with clearly acting on the basis of my Christian faith in a way which distinguishes me from most of my contemporaries who do not share that faith. But is there the same sort of difference between me and a secular humanist in the sphere of morality? If there is, it is certainly not such an immediately obvious one. The way in which such a difference is most commonly affirmed is by emphasizing that the basic characteristic of the moral life of the Christian is obedience to the will of God. 'All Christians,' writes H. P. Owen, 'would agree that for them morality consists in (or at least includes) obedience to the will of God.'[34] And Peter Baelz declares that 'obedience has traditionally been considered a fundamental, perhaps the fundamental, Christian virtue'.[35] This traditional emphasis on obedience to the will of God has been for a long time the target of trenchant criticism from opponents of Christianity. The objections are not without force. They involve challenges both to its moral appropriateness and to its practical possibility. The emphasis on obedience attracts the charge that such a morality is 'infantile', that it represents a refusal to grow up and accept the responsibility that appertains to mature human life.[36] And when Christians, like Kierkegaard, use the story of Abraham's sacrifice of Isaac to show that the command of God can rightly override even our deepest moral convictions, it has to be admitted that they provide ample occasion for such protests.[37] But the objection, like the objection to God's apparently vain desire for human adoration, derives from an unjustifiably anthropomorphic view of God. If the language of obedience were to be taken at its face value, we would have to acknowledge with Ian Ramsey that such a 'theory appears to speak of God as though he were some oriental potentate, Headmaster or Sergeant-Major'.[38] But the account of religious language and of God's relation to the world that I have been developing so far is sufficient answer to that particular objection, and the difficulty need not detain us. But the second objection is more serious. The more easily we dispose of the complaint that Christian morality is infantile in form, the harder it is to show that the idea of obedience to the will of God has any specific content which might constitute a distinctive contribution of Christian faith to the issues of morality.

At first sight the problem may not seem insuperable. The commands of God, we may claim, do not come to us in the arbitrary manner that a naive reading of the Abraham story might suggest. In scripture they are integrally related to and grow out of the revealed character of God. The Ten Commandments are not simply dictates brought down from the heights of Mount Sinai; they are presented as the appropriate human response to the God who has revealed himself in the saving activity of the Exodus (Exod. 20.2f.). The so-called 'ethical prophets' do not make unsubstantiated ethical demands; 'their standard,' as Norman Snaith put it, 'was what they themselves knew of the very Nature of God Himself . . . Knowledge of God came first, and the understanding of right action second'.[39] The moral injunctions of the Pauline letters follow after and are grounded in Paul's understanding of the revealed grace of God. So it seems not unreasonable to claim that there is a revealed will of God, which does not ride roughshod over our moral convictions, though it may enlarge and modify them through the process of its revelation. And if that be so, will that not provide something both distinctive and binding about Christian morality?

It is an attractive picture, but also a vulnerable one. For how is this revealed character or revealed will of God known to us? If it is to provide us with new and distinctive moral insights, then it must be possible for us to know it as the will of God by means which do not involve our moral judgment as a part of the process of recognition. Older views of scriptural authority allowed for revelation of that kind. But such a position is no longer possible. The issue can be neatly illustrated by an example from the Old Testament. In the Second Book of Samuel (24.1ff.), a story is told of how God incited David to number the people of Israel and then punished him for doing so. The First Book of Chronicles (21.1ff.) records the same story, but ascribes the original inciting of David not to God but to Satan. What was the source of the change? Not, surely, some revised communiqué from the heavenly court changing the ascription of responsibility, like the revised communiqués of an embarrassed political authority today. Is it not rather the outcome of a developing moral sense that could no longer accept the ascription of such morally unjustifiable conduct to God? The example is trivial, but the principle is far-reaching. The revealed will of God is not made known to us in a way that bypasses our moral judgment; our moral sense is one of the faculties by which we judge what is and what is not God's will. That will cannot therefore function as an independent source of moral knowledge.

This principle applies not just to the teaching of scripture in general. It applies to the most promising source of moral enlightenment for the Christian – the teaching of Jesus himself. Those who hold to a strong view of Jesus as incarnate Son of God might seem to be in a position to hope that there at last they may be able to find a supplementary source of moral direction for the Christian. But even then a twofold difficulty remains. For, asks Hughes, 'can we come to believe this of Jesus of Nazareth' (i.e. that he is incarnate Son of God) 'unless we have already satisfied ourselves that the life of Jesus of Nazareth was morally admirable – satisfied ourselves on *independent* grounds?'[40] Owen seeks to qualify the extent of the implications of Hughes' argument. He suggests that such a process need only involve our accepting 'the *mass* (of Christ's teaching) through the immediate assent of conscience' and that that might therefore leave a further area of teaching on matters about which our conscience was uncertain which it would be reasonable to accept on authority. But even in relation to such a restricted sphere of potentially authoritative teaching, the second difficulty would still operate. Could we, with our understanding of how the gospel tradition has come down to us, be sure that such teaching was the express teaching of the incarnate Son of God? So Owen has finally to acknowledge that 'whether there are in fact any elements in the (critically established) teaching of Jesus that can be thus accepted "on authority" is extremely doubtful'.[41]

These arguments should not be understood to rule out the significance of scripture or of the teaching of Jesus for the moral life of the Christian. All that it is designed to do is to show that we do not have there a declaration of the will of God, operating independently of that moral sense that is common to mankind as a whole. There can be little doubt that Moses, Isaiah, Jesus and Paul, all made substantial contributions to the development of our moral awareness. But the form in which their teaching comes to us is not such that we can accept it as morally binding, simply on the ground that they taught it or that God is believed to have inspired their teaching. In every case their teaching comes to us in forms that are neither wholly clear, consistent or convincing. We have to use our moral judgment to determine at what points and in what respects it is morally binding on us.

Nor should this be cause for surprise. Christ has traditionally been understood not only as a personally pre-existent Son disclosing the secrets of the Father; he has been seen also as the embodiment of the Logos or reason of God which enlightens everyone, as the personification of that Wisdom which is the source of all true discernment in the world. What such a saviour teaches must therefore be consistent with what is in principle accessible to every person by virtue of his or her constitution as a human being. So traditional Christian moral teaching has spoken not only of obedience to the revealed will of God but also of a 'natural law' by which men and women are able, as Christ is reported to have required of them, 'to judge of themselves what is right' (Luke 12.57). We ought not therefore to assume that the fact of Christianity's deep concern with ethics and with moral action necessarily involves its being able to offer some special and different source of moral knowledge. Nor should it be a matter for concern should it prove that it does not. With John Macquarrie, 'I see nothing threatening in the possibility that the foundations of Christian morality may be the same as the foundations of the moralities associated with other faiths or with non-religious beliefs'.[42] This is in fact the view taken by many of those mainly Catholic moral theologians who have been particularly critical of the search for a basis for ethics in the revealed will of God. 'Human morality (natural law) and Christian morality are *materially* identical,' writes McCormick, and goes on to claim an informed consensus for that judgment: 'This is what nearly everyone (e.g., Fuchs, Aubert, Macquarrie, Rahner) are saying these days'.[43] What is binding on the Christian is what is binding on human beings as human beings. In summarizing Aubert's views, he puts the matter more explicitly still in traditional natural law terms by speaking of 'a *material* identity between Christian moral demands and those perceivable by reason'.[44]

But how viable a road forward does such an approach offer? For if natural law has an honourable place in the history of Christian thought, that history also serves to make clear its problematic character. Is human nature sufficiently constant to serve as the basis of unchanging moral truths? And even if we should decide that it is, can we derive from it moral judgments with any significant content to them by the operation of reason alone? Can it not be shown that those who thought themselves able to do so have in fact infiltrated more particular assumptions into the premises of their arguments than the claimed form of argumentation permits? The problems are immense, and recent emphasis on the historical character of human existence, together with the relativizing implications of the sociology of knowledge, have only served to add to their difficulty. Would not therefore to fall back on natural law be to fall back on a broken reed? The fact that it would be likely to lead to a greater emphasis on the limitations of our moral insights would be no great loss. We have more than enough examples of the assertion of rival and incompatible Christian moral certainties. But it seems reasonable to ask that it should be able to offer us some positive guidance, however limited. Yet its ability to do so remains highly questionable. Even one of its supporters acknowledges that 'the dictates of natural law may be, are and may be expected to be a matter about which there is the utmost confusion and disagreement'.[45] One is tempted to say that with friends like that, what need has the theory of critics? It does not seem as if we are going to be any better off with an appeal to natural law than with an appeal to the revealed will of God in scripture. In neither case does it appear as if specific moral direction is likely to be forthcoming.

Yet there is, I believe, more to be said for this second approach. The term 'natural law' is unfortunate. The word 'natural' tends to suggest a conceptuality that works in terms of a contrast between 'nature' and 'super-nature', and the word 'law', something that ought to provide the kind of directives associated with positive law. Neither of these implications is helpful. George Woods describes the use of the word 'natural' in this context as 'depressingly uninformative' and the use of the word 'law' as approaching 'the limits of analogical propriety'.[46] But much of what contemporary appeal to it is concerned to emphasize can be better expressed in terms of an appeal to human experience.[47] That emphasis can be spelt out in a two-fold form. In the first place, there is the recognition that there are certain basic characteristics written into the context of human life which mean that we cannot simply make of it whatever we choose. However little we may be able to spell them out, it is important that we should acknowledge that they exist, that, in a phrase of McCormick's, 'man's being is the basis of the norms of his becoming'.[48] Such a recognition will affect the seriousness and the style of our reflection on present experience as we seek to make decisions about the future direction of human living. But the second emphasis is an equally serious recognition of historicity, change and becoming as fundamental features of human experience. It is this that has often been lacking from earlier conceptions of natural law.[49] Even if man's being provides the *basis* for the norms of his becoming, it should not be understood to prescribe the precise form that the becoming should take. The point is made strongly by Ryan, when he says that 'to be human involves being in a world-for-man which is very largely of man's own making'.[50] For example, it is undoubtedly the case that some agreed form of social interaction and of sexual behaviour is essential to a genuinely human form of existence, but that does not imply that there is only one such form that every society or cultural tradition ought to have developed and agreed upon, or that that which has been agreed upon should necessarily be regarded as permanent.

The direction in which such reflections point us is one which sees moral actions as having a dual structure. They must incorporate both a recognition of how things are and a decision about the direction in which we choose to change them. In other words, they are a matter partly of discovery and partly of creation. The picture to which we are being led here is identical with that which emerged in our earlier discussion of religious language.[51] The similarity is not coincidental. We began this discussion with the aim of trying to give more precision to the concept of the personal, of the truly human. And if we are right in seeing the human as an open concept, with a variety of creative possibilities before it, then it cannot be adequately delineated in terms of its original or present constitution, whether that be given by divine declaration or by the careful consideration of human reason. The grasp of future possibilities is a matter of vision, something dependent on the faculty of the imagination. And if it is essential for morality to understand the concept of the human in terms of what it might become in the future, then morality cannot ultimately be independent of some overall vision of a broadly religious kind.

The primary mode by which the imagination fulfils this role

is by the creation of myths and stories. 'Story-telling,' it has been said, 'is the original and indispensable way we articulate our understanding of the world and the self.'[52] That is true not only in a general way but of each individual. 'A man's sense of his own identity seems largely determined by the kind of story which he understands himself to have been enacting through the events of his career, the story of his life.'[53] This kind of stress is not limited to Christian writing. The importance of the story in the particular sphere of moral philosophy is widely recognized. Ronald Hepburn, for example, sees it as a much needed supplement to the dominating influence of the 'rule-obedience' model.[54] And Iris Murdoch stresses its importance not just in relation to the theoretical understanding of morality but in particular instances where moral decision is required. 'There are,' she writes, 'moments when situations are unclear and what is needed is not a renewed attempt to specify the facts, but a fresh vision which may be derived from a "story".'[55]

The understanding of Christian faith that I have been trying to develop is well fitted to fulfil such a role. Its scriptures have a markedly narrative character. They tell a cosmic story of God's purpose for the world, with a variety of pictures of what the consummation of that purpose might mean for humankind. Its central figure is both a story-teller, and one about whom a number of different life-stories are told. So it embodies a rich vein of story-telling in relation to which our varied life situations can be seen. Moreover, the ineradicable admixture of the historical and the imaginative in scripture, which at times is experienced as an embarrassment, is for this purpose a positive advantage. It is in these terms that the pioneering moral insights of Moses and Isaiah, of Jesus and Paul are best understood. They derived their insights from a vision of life grounded in the story of God's dealings with his people as they knew it, and those insights in their turn contributed to the further imaginative development of the story. In the same sort of way for me too the story of faith contributes imaginatively to an understanding of the human and so indirectly to the determination of moral action. The role that the story fulfils is heuristic rather than probative; it suggests possibilities rather than justifies decisions. Its suggestions need to be tested, for as history reveals, they may be suggestions of a Herrenvolk as well as of a liberation. And for the work of testing the Christian needs to draw on all the resources that critical reason has been able to develop. In terms of providing clear moral injunctions, the approach through imaginative story is as inconclusive as the other approaches we have considered. Its advantage is that it offers an alternative conception of what it is that specifically Christian faith has to offer in relation to the moral life.

I set out on an attempt to give some greater precision to the concept of the human. The results are depressingly meagre. No available approach seems able to lift us out of the morass of generality and vagueness. But if it is part of the church's role 'to *change* the world as it is in the direction of God's purpose for its future', is not something more required than the offer of an imaginative vision? Indeed it is. But the importance of the vision must not be underestimated. The effectiveness in strictly political terms of Martin Luther King's 'dream' is witness to that fact. But though important at that level, it is not sufficient. If change is to be effected, actions are needed of a highly specific nature, in particular of a specifically political nature. Christianity cannot accept for a moment that its concern is limited to some other eternal realm. But how does it function at the level of practical, political action?

Political action is always complex. The temptation of the politician is either to abandon his or her vision or to oversimplify the issues. It is the latter temptation to which the Christian is particularly prone to succumb. The answer is not to be ashamed of the vision: 'where there is no vision, the people perish' (Prov. 29.18). It is rather to give even closer attention to the contingent factors relating to its possible application. But it is not easy to do justice to both at the same time. And here it seems important to draw a relative distinction (and it cannot be more than relative) between the role of the church as a whole and that of the individual Christian or informal group of Christians.

The church is a society whose institutional character is necessary but ambiguous; necessary because some form of institutional framework is required for personal flourishing, and ambiguous because that institutional form inevitably militates against some aspects of the freedom and the universality which are integral to the purpose of the church.[56] Its greatest danger is to become a society with clear-cut boundaries, defining itself by its position over against other societies. Yet to act as a society directly within the political sphere contributes to just such an attitude. And if the theoretical reasons against such a role do not convince, the historical record of the church's participation in the political arena should give us pause. But that is not to deny the church any role at all in relation to the political sphere. The need for a continual re-pristination of the vision and of a prophetic challenge to our failure to live by it remains. 'The characteristic function of the pulpit,' writes Daniel Jenkins, 'in relation to politics should be to raise questions and to promote self-criticism rather than to do what politicians of every kind look for, which is to provide support for their own cause.' It is an activity, Jenkins goes on to claim, that 'can do much to deliver political activity from the demons which always hover around it and which can so quickly make it totalitarian'.[57]

Yet if that were all, the church would rightly be open to the charge of escapism, of evasion of responsibility, of offering only the kind of spectators' advice that is rightly scorned. But it is not all. If the pulpit is here a symbol for the public and official utterances of the church, it is a small minority of the members of the church who speak from pulpits. The church should encourage its members to play a full and active part in the political arena.[58] It should recognize that in doing so they will not only differ from one another in judgment, but also make serious mistakes. Neither the goal, nor the way to the goal, is ever unmistakably clear. But the church should provide a forum within which men and women are able to test out both their ideals and their more immediate objectives with one another in the light of that unclear but challenging Christian story. Moreover, the taking of political responsibility, with all the risks that are an inevitable corollary of it, is to be seen not as something in which the church reluctantly acquiesces, but as a concomitant part of what is involved in living out that for which the church exists.

There have in the past been sections of the church which have tried to make some aspect of moral conduct a defining characteristic of the church. The history of such puritan sects makes depressing reading. For what was often a noble ideal in origin easily becomes a strait-jacket in practice. For moral ideals and moral action can only become defining characteristics of the church in normal circumstances if they are narrowed down to some clearly definable set of external actions. This is what happened in the classic case of Donatist concentration on holiness in terms of the avoidance of all compromise in time of persecution. In his rejection of the Donatist position, Augustine was concerned to insist that holiness was indeed an essential mark of the church, but not one that could be used now to distinguish the wheat from the tares. It was rather an eschatological mark, something by which God alone could make such a divison at the end of the world.[59] Augustine's position inevitably runs the risk that the moral demands of Christian faith will be regarded as less binding than they really are. Such a danger is intensified when other aspects of what is involved in response to the gospel go on being treated as definitive. Certain doctrinal beliefs have continued to function as definitive of the church, not only because they were seen as logically prior to the moral demands, but also because they were thought to be given with an unequivocalness lacking in the moral case and to be something which it was always open to fallible men and women to accept whatever the failures in practice into which sinful human weakness might lead them.

I have been arguing that belief and worship, moral judgment and moral action stand on a much more equal footing in respect of the way of faith and the nature of the church. In aiming to restore them to a better balance in the understanding of Christian faith, our aim should not be to reintroduce, like some modern day Donatists, certain forms of moral belief or action as defining marks of church membership. But it should be to recognize the parallelism of belief and action in this regard. The appropriate understanding of God made known in Jesus Christ is as problematic as the understanding of the moral demands which faith lays upon us. Making the acceptance of particular forms of belief the test of church membership runs the same risks as the insistence on specific forms of moral action. And the recognition of an openness in relation to expressed beliefs no more implies an indifferentism with regard to truth than Augustine's rejection of Donatism implies an indifferentism with regard to holiness. What we are called to as Christians is a continuing task of critical reflection on the traditions of Christian belief and moral understanding, and a practical commitment to the way of life and action to which that reflection directs us.

7

God as Spirit

The choice of the title of Professor Lampe's Bampton Lectures[1] as the title of my final chapter is not primarily intended as a tribute to their author. But it can most appropriately fulfil that role nonetheless. For Geoffrey Lampe embodied in his own person that which this book is designed to demonstrate at a more theoretical level – namely, that it is possible to combine a radically critical stance towards many of the traditional formulations of church doctrine with a life of faith in and for the church. For he was widely known and loved not only as a man of faith but as a man of the church. Yet one cannot challenge the hallowed structures of belief much more daringly than he did on the last page of his Bampton Lectures when he wrote: 'I believe that the Trinitarian model is in the end less satisfactory for the articulation of our basic Christian experience than the unifying concept of God as Spirit.'[2]

But the primary reason for the choice of the title is its intrinsic suitability. For the question that remains to be tackled in this final chapter is whether the understanding of God implicit in all that has been written so far is one that stands recognizably within historical Christian tradition. At an earlier stage I took the description of God as 'Father' as characteristic of traditional speech about God and sought to explore the rich imagistic power of that designation.[3] But there are features of its use which become problematic if we try to make it the primary co-ordinating concept for our reflective understanding of God.

In the first place God's fatherhood, as we saw earlier, may refer either to an internal relation to the Son within the Godhead itself or to God's relation to the created order as a whole. Yet in traditional thought those relationships are of radically different kinds. In the one case the implication of the term is community of being; in the other it is origination of something of an altogether different order of being. However valuable such ambiguity of reference may be for the purposes of religious suggestibility, it is liable to be confusing where the primary aim is conceptual clarity. Secondly, the use of the term 'Father' tends to suggest an individual person. Such a suggestion, it would widely be agreed, needs to be qualified by the use of other less individualistically personal terms. With the help of multiple imagery this corrective process is not too hard to achieve. But once again it is less easy to do if the term 'Father' is regarded as a primary co-ordinating concept for our thought about God. Finally the male character of the term is a further disadvantage for its use in so dominating a role. No doubt all these potential difficulties can be overcome if in the course of reflection we remain attentive to the dangers. Selecting a single co-ordinating concept for our thought about God is not a matter of choosing between a right and a wrong answer; it is a matter of which choice is more or less appropriate. But the shortcomings of the Father image for that role are substantial. When the necessary corrections and qualifications have been made, we would be left with a somewhat emasculated image. It is at least worthy of consideration that the similarly biblical and traditional imagery of God as spirit may better serve our purpose.

God is spirit (John 4.24) – not *a* spirit, as if he were one of a class, as the Authorized Version translation and the introductory sentence to Morning and Evening Prayer in the 1928 Prayer Book have accustomed generations of English-speaking Christians to hear and say. Root meanings of *pneuma*, the Greek word for 'spirit', are wind and breath, as the author of the Fourth Gospel was well aware. And that grounding of the imagery continues to play a role in the later language of the church. Hymns speak of the Spirit at Pentecost sometimes as a 'rushing mighty wind', sometimes as 'soft as breath of even'. Like other images, it unites ideas that at a more straightforward level are felt to be incompatible, and thereby points to an elusiveness about the divine activity which cannot be appropriately conveyed in other than symbolic terms. But it is not only the physical entities of wind and breath that lie behind the application of the word to God. Indeed, when the application is more directly to God and less to the effects of his action in the world, it is not they that are of primary importance. Even at the non-religious level, the word 'spirit' is most commonly used with a non-physical referent, as when we speak of the spirit of the age. But it is not such sub-personal usage either that gives it its especial appropriateness as a designation of God. Both in biblical and contemporary usage we speak of the human spirit, indicating thereby that which makes us most truly and fully personal. In biblical usage, 'spirit' is particularly used of men and women in their relation to God. It is not always clear whether particular biblical writers are working with a tripartite understanding of human nature (as body, soul and spirit) or with a bipartite understanding, according to which 'spirit' can only rightly be used of those whose lives have become consciously oriented to God in faith. Commentators, both early and contemporary, disagree about Paul's usage of the term.[4] This very uncertainty is indicative of the fact that spirit is not to be thought of as just one part of our constitution as human beings. Rather it is a way of speaking of men and women in their potential or actual relationship to God. In more modern terminology, 'spirit' is roughly equivalent to the human capacity for self-transcendence, that power by which we not only exist as finite human beings but also in our consciousness of ourselves as such may be said to transcend our finitude. Karl Rahner speaks of man reaching beyond his finiteness and experiencing 'himself as a transcendent being, as spirit.'[5] In other words, at the human level the word indicates not only the fact of our existence as persons, but that by which we can, as it were, stand back from ourselves and be aware of ourselves as persons. Thus Kierkegaard can begin the main body of *Sickness unto Death* with the words: 'Man is spirit. But what is spirit? Spirit is the self. But what is the self? The self is a relation which relates itself to its own self.'[6] But this is to put the point in too individualistic a manner. For it is primarily in our relatedness to the world and particularly to other persons that the germ of this capacity for self-transcendence is to be found. So John Taylor can write: 'My spirit, therefore, is never uniquely mine as are my body, my life, my individuality. It resides only in my relatedness to some other. Spirit is that which lies between, making both separateness and conjunction real.'[7]

It is this connotation of the word at the human level that makes it so appropriate an analogue for our most basic speech about God. For there are two fundamental characteristics of the conception of God that we are stumblingly attempting to articulate. In the first place it must be a profoundly personal concept, yet one that bursts the restrictive bounds of what it is to be an individual person as we know that in our finite human experience. And secondly it is God in relation to us with which we have to do, for any knowledge of God that we have is so inextricably bound up with our particular experience of him that what we say about him can never be wholly separated out from the limiting and distorting prism of that contingent experience. These two concerns find expression in the language of spirit. For it speaks at the same time of a personal, but not limitedly individual, transcendence and of an essential relatedness. This is true even of its most traditional use in, for example, the Old Testament, as Geoffrey Lampe brings out: ' "Spirit" characterizes the very nature of God in his transcendence, that which God is and creatures are not: "The Egyptians are men (*adam*) and not God (*el*), their horses are flesh (*basar*) and not spirit (*ruach*)." Yet for the most part in the Old Testament the Spirit is God in his outreach towards men, interacting with their created spirits and integrating their thoughts and emotions and wills with his own.'[8] And that is also, as we have seen, the thrust of much contemporary reflection about 'spirit' in human experience. For it is that which makes a person most fully a person, precisely by taking him out of the confines of his individual self through his or her relationship and communion with others.

It is precisely this understating of the word 'spirit' that has made it appeal so strongly to many contemporary theologians. It is John Taylor's conviction, for example, that the contradictions which do so much to undermine the vitality of our belief in God will 'begin to resolve themselves when the Holy Spirit becomes so central to our thoughts about God and about man that whenever the name "God" is used our minds go first to the Spirit, and not last'.[9] His analysis of the problem is valid; but his proposed solution does not go far enough. What is called for is not a reversal of priorities within our understanding of the Trinity. Rather it is no longer to allow the concept of 'Spirit' to be appropriated as the name for one person of the Trinity, but rather to put it to work as the primary determinant for all our reflective apprehension of God.[10] Even so, 'spirit' is not, of course, a direct description of the nature of God. The term is, in Tillich's language, a symbol like all other statements about him. It is rooted in our experience of spirit in ourselves and made possible by our understanding of spirit as a dimension of human life.[11] But in locating the ground of our usage there (rather than simply in the more primitive meaning of *pneuma* as wind or breath), we are acknowledging that our language in this case is less stretched than with most other language that we use in speaking of God. We have every reason therefore to expect that it may prove the best available language for co-ordinating our affirmations about him.

The most fundamental issue with which we were grappling in the earlier part of this book was the question of God's action in the world. One does not need to take a strictly mechanistic (and thereby untenable) view of the world to experience this as extremely problematic; one has only to be aware of the kind of regularities in the functioning of the world which modern knowledge has disclosed to us. With such an awareness God's action in the world is bound to appear problematic to anyone whose faith envisages it not just as peripheral or occasional but as the most basic reality of life. The primary model with which we began and which proved to be at the heart of so many of the problems was that of God as agent, conceived after the pattern of our own experience as individual personal agents. But if we take God as spirit rather than as personal agent as our basic model, we may be helped to move one step nearer towards a more appropriate conceptuality. In thinking of God as spirit, our image is still profoundly personal. Its starting point is the inwardness and relatedness of personal being. Its stress is not so much on active agency as on the experience of being a person by virtue of our self-reflexive relation to ourselves and still more our relatedness to other persons. For there can be a rich communion between persons simply by their mutual presence to one another. Gabriel Marcel has given a careful philosophical account of this concept of 'presence'. He distinguishes between a purely physical and a deeper sense of 'presence'. In the first case

> a kind of physical, but merely physical, communication is possible; the image of the passing of messages between a reception point and an emission point . . . is in fact quite applicable here. Yet something essential is lacking. We might say that what we have with this person, who is in the room, but somehow not really present to us, is communication without communion: unreal communication, in a word. He understands what I say to him, but he does not understand *me*.

On the other hand

> when somebody's presence does really make itself felt, it can refresh my inner being; it reveals me to myself, it makes me

more fully myself than I should be if I were not exposed to its impact.[12]

Such a presence, he goes on to argue, 'can, in the last analysis, only be invoked or evoked'. It may at times be conjured up by the evocative power of poetry.[13] Moreover it is not barren; if we distinguish, as we should, creation from production, it has the power to create. We see it in the lives of those who 'by the radiance of charity and love shining from their being, . . . add a positive contribution to the invisible work which gives the human adventure the only meaning which can justify it'.[14]

The language with which Marcel speaks of our human inter-subjective experience bears many of the marks that we have seen to be characteristic of religious language. And in using it to help elucidate our understanding of God's relation to the world, we are not moving outside Marcel's own intentions. For he himself employs it in that way; it is his particular form of that appeal to human experience as ground for faith in God which we saw earlier to be so characteristic of contemporary theological reflection.[15] His philosophy has been described in a somewhat inelegant phrase as an 'analogy of presentiality' – a description which in its French form Marcel himself describes as 'très heureux'.[16] He acknowledges 'a "Presence" from which all other "presences" draw their life and worth'.[17] But in drawing on it in this way, we must be careful not to claim too much. In his book, *The Future of Belief*, Leslie Dewart suggests that it can replace traditional language about the being of God and resolve the problems associated with that language.[18] But if that is to overstate the case, nonetheless his book with its more directly theological application of Marcel's ideas points us in a valuable direction.

The correlation of 'spirit' and 'presence' has firm roots in the biblical tradition. 'Whither shall I go from thy spirit? Or whither shall I flee from thy presence?' (Ps. 139.7). God as spirit is God as present – present potentially at least in the full sense of that word that Marcel was attempting to evoke. And such language is peculiarly appropriate to that understanding of God's action which I earlier described as operating within the sphere of final rather than efficient causation.[19] It helps us, as reflective theology is intended to help us, to grasp better the direction in which the parabolic language of faith about God's transforming power is pointing us.

And it is not only in relation to the more general question of divine agency that the concept of God as spirit is of value. A central theme of Geoffrey Lampe's Bampton Lectures was that that concept enables us to do more justice, not less, to the intention of incarnational doctrine. In a bold reversal of the usual judgment, he argues that such an approach avoids the 'reductionism' to which the concept of a pre-existent Son 'reduces the real, socially and culturally conditioned, personality of Jesus'.[20] And it is able to do so without loss in terms of what is traditionally spoken of as his divine nature, precisely because 'inspiration' is not a lower level of divine indwelling than 'incarnation'. For inspiration is not 'an impersonal influence communicated to a human person externally by a remote deity'; rather it conveys 'the deeper meaning of a "real presence" of God himself'.[21]

But if the concept of God as spirit – and thereby of God's presence – can be of value for the understanding of the person of Christ, we may expect it to prove even more appropriate for our understanding of the church, for it is the church that is most closely linked with the doctrine of the Holy Spirit in traditional theology. And here once again it helps to formulate more clearly the conclusions to which our earlier discussion has led us. For I argued that the distinguishing mark of the church was not that it was the locus of any special activity on the part of God. I spoke of it rather, in Bill Vanstone's words, as the place where creative love is recognized as love.[22] God is always present as spirit. But for that presence to be 'presence' in the full sense of the word there is need for recognition and openness on the part of those to whom God is present. It is this recognition (provided it is real and not just formal) that makes God 'present' as spirit in the life of the church.

I have been trying to show how the concept of God as spirit points towards a way of understanding God that does substantial justice both to the main insights of traditional faith and to the critical challenges of contemporary reflection. Of course it is no panacea. It does not solve every intellectual problem or meet every religious need. On the intellectual side the coherence and intelligibility of the understanding it implies need to be tested as best we are able. But there are limits to our ability to test them. For there is no one metaphysic that is clearly the true one from the standpoint either of human reason or of Christian faith. What is important is that the work of critical testing goes on. It may lead us to modify our understanding of the implications of our image. I do not think it will turn out to show our use of the image itself to be inappropriate or absurd. On the religious side the image needs supplementing by other symbols and images. The primary advantage that I have been claiming for the image of God as spirit is its fruitfulness as a co-ordinating concept at a comparatively formal level of understanding. It is, as we have seen, not without value in terms of material content for the articulation of faith also. But other images which are less comprehensive in the range of their application may prove to have a richer imaginative content for the furtherance of the life of faith.

But first we need to take note of one other important advantage in the use of 'spirit' as a primary and controlling concept in our speech about God. It constitutes a standing prophetic challenge against all possible abuse of other imagery used of God. The original Johannine context of the affirmation 'God is spirit' was the conversation of Jesus with the woman at the well of Samaria (John 4.19, 24). The woman wants Jesus to pronounce on the rival claims of Mount Gerizim and Jerusalem to be the proper centre for the worship of God. In speaking of God as spirit and spirit as the essential characteristic of worship, Jesus rebuts the claim of any place, however rich in association and tradition, to an exclusive position in that regard. But the principle applies not only to places and buildings. It applies also to the language and imagery with which we speak of God in theology and in worship. No imagery, however tried and valued, can claim an absolute or permanent validity. It stands under the prophetic challenge of the primary affirmation of God as spirit. That apprehension serves to put all other imagery in a properly limited perspective. But other imagery remains important. The fact that it is open to the risk of abuse does not make it one whit the less necessary. For, as we have seen throughout, it is a feature of all religious language that those very characteristics from which it derives its creative potential have also a potential for being misunderstood.

What then is to be the source of this other imagery? Imagery cannot be conjured up at will. We may call for it, but will it, any more than the spirits from the vasty deep, come when we do call?[23] But we do not need to call, for it is there in the tradition. It is not always perfectly suited to our needs; but whatever its shortcomings on that score, there is always a substantial compensation in its traditional character. To agree, as I do, with Geoffrey Lampe, 'that the Trinitarian model is in the end less satisfactory for the articulation of our basic Christian experience than the unifying concept of God as Spirit' is not to deny the great value of that trinitarian model in the multiple imagery of our language about God. It represents a pattern into which my own critical reflection continually falls. It underlies the shape of this book as a whole in its triple concern with the religious dimension of ultimacy, the transforming significance of Jesus and the continuing life of the Christian community. It recurred again at the beginning of the last chapter in the discussion of worship with its evocation of mystery, its christological focus and its orientation in prayer towards the changing of the world.[24]

Does such a use of trinitarian language, such a relocation of the trinitarian symbols stand in genuine continuity with the trinitarian character of traditional Christian faith? That it embodies a shift in use and understanding is beyond dispute. But if the account of religious language for which I have argued is at all along the right lines, it is the kind of shift that is appropriate within a living tradition of thought and worship. For I have argued that all our language about God is the fruit of an imaginative construction that involves both disclosure and creation. Nor are we in a position to draw clear lines of demarcation to show where the one begins and the other ends. Only if the character of doctrine were understood in more exclusively disclosive terms, could the proposed change in the understanding of trinitarian symbolism be legitimately interpreted as a breach of continuity rather than as a development within a living tradition.

But in my judgment it is precisely that way of seeing and perpetuating our doctrinal heritage that is the greater danger to the life of faith. For to insist that the trinitarian symbolism is not only a valuable guide to reflection and worship but also disclosive of the essential nature of God himself embodies a claim to knowledge about the being of God that is hard to reconcile with the experiential and experimental character of faith. Moreover the traditional insistence that the trinitarian distinctions belong only to the internal life of God and that the activity of God in the world is always the activity of the one God (*opera trinitatis ad extra indivisa*) effectively removes the doctrine from the issue of God's relation to the world, which has been at the heart of our concern. And just because that is so, I want to claim that my counter-insistence on the creative element in the emergence of the symbolism and my consequent unwillingness to affirm it as something that can be known to be an unchanging truth about the nature of God himself in fact serves to enhance rather than to reduce both the religious character and the relevance of the doctrine.

The relation of faith and reason has been an uneasy one down the ages. Thorough-going fideists, who with Luther would dismiss reason as the 'devil's whore', are few in number today. Most Christians wish to claim that their own faith is reasonable, while remaining free to criticize as rationalist those whose reasoning takes them away from the forms of faith that they themselves embrace. In the past it was natural enough to apply the term 'rationalist' to those critics who questioned the hallowed formulations of the so-called 'deposit of faith'. For was not acceptance of that deposit an essential aspect of faith itself? And was not the readiness to criticize it evidence of an arrogant reliance on the critic's own unaided reasoning powers? But today it seems at least as appropriate to apply the term to some of the defenders of traditional forms or belief. For it is the claim to a sure knowledge of the truth of particular beliefs about God that seems (once it abandons a purely fideist position) to have to place an unwarranted confidence in the capacity of human reason to articulate knowledge about God. But such a way of putting the issue is liable to degenerate into unconstructive polemic. For the issue is not whether, but how, reason is to be used in relation to Christian faith. And the point that I want to emphasize, and to emphasize as a Christian theologian, is the limitation of that knowledge about God to which we can properly lay claim.

That insistence is one which seems to many to undermine precisely the possibility of that reasonable faith to which we aspire. I hope I have succeeded in showing why such a reaction is misconceived. For it is not a set of unquestioned beliefs that faith requires if it is to be properly grounded. It is rather the readiness continually to test, to review and where necessary to revise both the traditional affirmations of faith and its contemporary insights. And when I try to do that, I still find myself convinced of a personal reality at the source of things – one whose character of love is most fully evoked by the figure of Jesus in that parabolic way in which alone the ultimate can be articulated and whose presence is most fully evoked through life shared with others in the Christian community. For me at least (and how in such a matter can one speak for others?) the claims of such a faith on one's life is not weakened by the limitation of the claim to knowledge or by the continued questioning to which it has to be submitted.

Towards the end of one of the earlier works in which he grappled with the problem of the relation of divine grace and human free will, Augustine acknowledges that his reflections have not provided a full resolution of the sense of puzzlement to which the issue gives rise, and goes on to say:

> There remains indeed one profound mystery, why this suasion in one man is effective, in another not. If I am pressed to attempt its fathoming, I can think at the moment of only two answers that I should like to give: 'O the depth of the riches . . .' (Rom. 11.33) and, 'Is there any unrighteousness with God?' (Rom. 9.14). He whom the reply contents not may look for more instructed counsellors; but let him beware of finding such as are over-confident.[25]

The wisdom of that final warning was one which Augustine himself failed in the end to heed. For in his later years he became one of those whom his earlier reply failed to content, and found over-confident counsel in his own unqualified predestinarian teaching. But the principle enunciated in his earlier writing retains its validity. The appeal to mystery can be an evasion of proper critical questioning. But that is not its true implication. Augustine does not forbid those who are not contented with his own answer to look elsewhere. For while mystery warns us against the speciously attractive answers that would dissolve it, it also encourages us to continue with the looking, for we can never tell whether we have reached the limits of human understanding. Indeed it is to such a continued search for understanding that faith commits us.

NOTES

1. On Being a Christian Today

1. John Taylor, 'The Theological Basis of Interfaith Dialogue', in *Christianity and Other Religions*, ed. J. Hick and B. Hebblethwaite, Collins 1980, pp. 212–33, esp. pp. 224 and 226.

2. See my *The Making of Christian Doctrine*, Cambridge University Press 1967, pp. 8f., and the quotation there from G. Tyrrell, 'the dogmas of the Church . . . change their sense, if not necessarily their expression, with the ages to which they are expressed.'

3. See my *Explorations in Theology* 4, SCM Press 1979, p. 32.

4. Cf. *The Remaking of Christian Doctrine*, SCM Press 1974, p. 106, and *What is Theology?*, Oxford University Press 1976, p. 44.

5. K. Thomas, *Religion and the Decline of Magic*, Weidenfeld and Nicolson 1971, pp. 639f.

6. L. Bayly, *The Practice of Piety*, [53]1719, pp. 246f., and *The Diary of Ralph Josselin*, ed. A. Macfarlane, Oxford University Press 1976, p. 114. Both examples are cited by K. Thomas, op. cit., pp. 83–5.

7. G. W. H. Lampe, *God as Spirit*, Oxford University Press 1977, pp. 183f.

8. W. Pannenberg, 'Anthropology and the Question of God', in *Basic Questions in Theology* Vol. 3, SCM Press 1973, p. 87.

9. See especially B. Mitchell, *The Justification of Religious Belief*, Macmillan 1973.

10. W. Pannenberg, 'Speaking about God in the Face of Atheist Criticism', op. cit., p. 107.

11. I have already touched on the question of the understanding of the world in *The Remaking of Christian Doctrine*, p. 34.

12. Pannenberg, op. cit., 89–91.

13. See G. Kaufman, *God the Problem*, Harvard University Press 1972, pp. 33f.; D. Cupitt, *The Leap of Reason*, Sheldon Press 1976, pp. 65f.

14. See S. M. Ogden, *The Reality of God*, SCM Press 1967, p. 42.

15. See H. Küng, *Does God Exist?*, Collins 1980, especially pp. 460–77 and 570–5.

16. Ogden, op. cit., p. 43.

17. Ibid.

18. W. Pannenberg, 'Anthropology and the Question of God', in *Basic Questions in Theology* Vol. 3, p. 96. Elsewhere, however (in 'Types of Atheism and Their Theological Significance', op. cit., Vol. 2, p. 191), he seems to allow this approach something more like probative force. He writes: 'The modern metaphysics of man's subjectivity is conceivable only on the presupposition of a God.'

19. Cf. W. Pannenberg, *Theology and the Philosophy of Science*, Darton, Longman and Todd 1976, p. 288.

20. S. Evans, 'Towards a Christian Doctrine of Providence', in *Providence*, ed. M. Wiles, SPCK 1969, p. 91.

21. Art cit., p. 97, in acknowledged dependence on the work of John Macquarrie.

22. Op. cit., pp. 36–9.

2. *The Language of Faith: Creation and Disclosure*

1. S. Prickett, 'What do the Translators Think They are Up To?', *Theology* LXX, November 1977, p. 407 (italics original). My agreement with the principle that Mr Prickett expresses so forcefully should not be taken to imply agreement with all the strictures he levels against recent translations of the Bible.

2. The precise usage of the words 'image' and 'symbol' vary with different writers. The distinction used here is one suggested by P. Wheelwright, *Metaphor and Reality*, Indiana University Press 1962, p. 93, where he writes: 'When an image is employed as metaphor only once, in a flash of insight, it cannot accurately be said to function symbolically. It acquires a symbolic nature when, with whatever modifications, it undergoes or is considered capable of undergoing recurrence.'

3. Cf. Theodore Jennings Jr, *Introduction to Theology*, SPCK 1977, where Part I, 'The "What" of Theological Reflection', is divided into four chapters entitled 'The Imagination', 'The Range of Imagination', 'The Religious Imagination', and 'The Christian Mythos'.

4. For a lively account of the relation between poetry and theology see 'Poetic Truth', in A. M. Farrer, *Reflective Faith*, SPCK 1972, pp. 24–38.

5. N. Lash, 'Interpretation and Imagination', in *Incarnation and Myth*, ed. M. Goulder, SCM Press 1979, p. 21.

6. Cf. P. Wheelwright, *The Burning Fountain*, Indiana University Press 1968, p. 88. 'Poetry and expressive language in general have, to be sure, their own kind of precision, but it is essentially different from the precision of literal language, even though there is no clear line of cleavage between them . . . We cannot ask whether one type of language is *more* precise than the other, we can only try to understand and accept their different kinds of precision' (italics original).

7. M. Warnock, 'Imagination – Aesthetic and Religious', *Theology* LXXXIII, November 1980, p. 408 (italics original).

8. P. Ricoeur, 'Creativity in Language: Word, Polysemy, Metaphor', *Philosophy Today*, Summer 1973, pp. 110f.; cited by S. TeSelle, *Speaking in Parables*, SCM Press 1975, p. 56.

9. Max Black, 'More about Metaphors', in *Metaphor and Thought*, ed. A. Ortony, Cambridge University Press 1979, p. 39 (italics original).

10. J. Maritain, 'The Frontiers of Poetry', in *Art and Scholasticism*, London 1946, pp. 75f.; cited by Rowan Williams, 'Poetic and Religious Imagination', *Theology* LXXX, May 1977, p. 179.

11. P. Wheelwright, *Metaphor and Reality*, p. 51.

12. Eliseo Vivas, *Creation and Discovery*, Noonday Press 1955, p. x (italics original).

13. Ibid., p. 89.

14. M. Black, op. cit., p. 41.

15. Brian Gerrish has written of Troeltsch's view of faith: 'Although faith's language is supplied by fantasy, faith is still "cognitive" ... A strong conviction of reality distinguishes faith from the free play of the artistic imagination' ('Ernst Troeltsch and the Possibility of a Historical Theology', in *Ernst Troeltsch and the Future of Theology*, ed. J. P. Clayton, Cambridge University Press 1976, p. 133). The words can be given a wider application to the understanding of faith in general.

16. I have approached the discussion of religious language by means of comparison with poetic language. Very similar conclusions could also be drawn by way of comparison with the use of models in science. Cf. Ian Barbour, *Myths, Models and Paradigms*, SCM Press 1974, pp. 7 and 69, where he speaks of models in both science and religion as 'partial and provisional ways of imagining what is not observable', 'symbolic representations of aspects of the world which are not directly accessible to us', fulfilling 'both cognitive and non-cognitive functions.'

17. P. Slater, 'Parables, Analogues and Symbols', *Religious Studies* 4, October 1968, pp. 33f.

18. See pp. 4–5 above.

19. H. R. Schlette, *Towards a Theology of Religions*, Burns and Oates 1966, p. 112.

20. P. Tillich, *Dynamics of Faith*, Allen and Unwin 1957, p. 52.

21. See n. 15 above.

22. The New Testament tends to restrict the use of 'Father' to the latter two categories. But the first two have also been a regular feature of Christian language from at least the second century.

23. R. Tennant, 'The Impossibility of Being a Theologian', *Theology* LXIV, December 1961, p. 504. I have commented on Mr Tennant's article more fully in my *What is Theology?*, Oxford University Press 1976, pp. 58ff.

24. Cf. P. Tillich, *Systematic Theology* Vol. 1, Nisbet 1953, p. 266: 'The history of religions is full of dead symbols which have been killed not by a

scientific criticism of assumed superstitions but by a religious criticism of religion.'

25. E.g. Ian Ramsey, *Models of Divine Activity*, SCM Press 1973, p. 58: 'talk about God's activity must be literal and univocal.' This was a point on which he laid great stress in the last conversation I had with him, shortly before his death. For criticism of his position on this issue, see Brian Hebblethwaite, 'Providence and Divine Action', in *Religious Studies* 14, 2, June 1978, p. 228.

26. P. Tillich, 'The Meaning and Justification of Religious Symbols', in *Religious Experience and Truth*, ed. S. Hook, Oliver and Boyd 1962, pp. 8f.

3. The Language of Faith: Claims of Identity

1. W. K. Wimsatt, *The Verbal Icon*, Methuen 1970, pp. 69–83.

2. P. Wheelwright, *The Burning Fountain*, Indiana University Press 1968, pp. 33f. The term 'metaphoric imagination' of the 1954 edition is replaced by the less euphonious, if more precise, term 'compositive imagination' in the revised 1968 edition.

3. Mary Warnock emphasizes the same two things in her account of Coleridge's view of imagination. 'Imagination is that with which we actively bring together different perceptions, to show their essential unity. It is also that with which we perceive individual things, and take them as significant of the universal ideas which lie behind them' (*Imagination*, Faber 1976, p. 100).

4. P. Wheelwright, op. cit., p. 98 (italics original).

5. L. Lévy-Bruhl, *The Notebooks on Primitive Mentality*, Blackwell 1975, pp. 7–11, 99–101, 126f.

6. Ibid., p. 103.

7. Ibid., pp. 125f.

8. Robin Horton, 'Paradox and Explanation', in *Philosophy of the Social Sciences* 3, 1973, p. 292.

9. E. Evans-Pritchard, *Nuer Religion*, Oxford University Press 1956, pp. 139f.

10. Ibid., pp. 128, 142, 203.

11. J. Skorupski, *Symbol and Theory*, Cambridge University Press 1976, p. 221.

12. See J. Skorupski, 'Science and Traditional Religious Thought', in *Philosophy of the Social Sciences* 3, 1973, p. 218.

13. M. Douglas, *Natural Symbols*, Barrie and Rockliff: The Cresset Press 1970, pp. 46f.

14. W. J. O'Shea, *Sacraments of Initiation*, Prentice-Hall Inc. 1966.

15. J. Skorupski, *Symbol and Theory*, p. 218. Cf. also his 'Science and Traditional Religious Thought' (n. 12 above), pp. 107–10.

16. M. Douglas, op. cit., p. 49.

17. J. Skorupski, *Symbol and Theory*, p. 220.

18. *Thinking about the Eucharist: Papers by Members of the Church of England Doctrine Commission*, SCM Press 1972, p. 56.

19. John 6.51–63. Some scholars attribute these different emphases to different sources, but I see no necessity for such suggestions.

20. See J. N. D. Kelly, *Early Christian Doctrines*, A. & C. Black 1958, pp. 211–14, 440–9.

21. See E. Schillebeeckx, *The Eucharist*, Sheed and Ward 1968, pp. 90–3.

22. Ibid., p. 104.

23. Ibid., p. 131; pp. 137f.

24. For Procter and Frere it was the last straw, whereby 'English religion reached its low water mark' (see F. Procter and W. H. Frere, *A New History of the Book of Common Prayer*, Macmillan 1902, p. 85).

25. *Scottish Liturgies of James VI*, ed. G. W. Sprott, Edmonston and Douglas 1871, p. 72.

26. Schillebeeckx, op. cit., pp. 134–6.

27. Augustine, Sermon 272.

28. E. L. Mascall, *Christ, the Christian and the Church*, Longmans 1946, pp. 161f. Cf. also p. 112: 'While it contains of course an element of metaphor, the description of the Church as the Body of Christ is to be taken ontologically and realistically.'

29. Cf. J. A. Baker, 'The Myth of the Church', in *What About the New Testament?*, ed. M. Hooker and C. Hickling, SCM Press 1975, p. 171.

30. J. A. T. Robinson, *The Body*, SCM Press 1952, p. 51 (italics original).

31. Ibid., p. 10; id., *Redating the New Testament*, SCM Press 1976, pp. 62f.

32. For well-argued criticism along these lines see E. Best, *One Body in Christ*, SPCK 1955, pp. 98–101.

33. A. Dulles, *Models of the Church*, Gill and Macmillan 1976, p. 51. The reference is to Karl Pelz, *Der Christ als Christus*, which Dulles has mentioned earlier on p. 48. See also J. A. Baker, art. cit., pp. 165–77.

34. M. Schmaus, *Dogma 4 – The Church*, Sheed and Ward 1972, p. 53.

35. C. C. J. Webb, *Problems in the Relations of God and Man*, Nisbet 1911, p. 231 (italics original).

36. H. R. Niebuhr, *The Responsible Self*, Harper and Row 1963, p. 155. The words quoted are part of a discussion of 'the symbolic form of Jesus Christ' and the immediately preceding words are: 'The symbol is not a mere figure of speech. Symbol and reality participate in each other.'

37. The policy statement is dated October 1968, and is cited in *Christian Aid in the World of 1973*, p. 12. I owe this reference, and other helpful comments on the interpretation of Matthew 25, to my colleague, John Fenton. Cf. Paul Oestreicher in *The Guardian*, Saturday 9 December 1978: 'When human rights are denied to any human being they are being denied to God himself. That is the message of the parable of the last judgment.'

38. K. Rahner, *Foundations of Christian Faith*, Darton, Longman and Todd 1978, pp. 448–59.

39. Ibid.

40. Luke 10.27; Deut. 6.5; Lev. 19.18; Luke 10.30–37.

41. 'A Christian Basis for Ethics', *Heythrop Journal*, Vol. XIII, January 1972, pp. 27–43; see esp. p. 41. For a fuller development of this theme see pp. 103–12 below.

42. One of Tolstoi's *Twenty-Three Tales*, written in 1885.

43. M. Green, *The Truth of God Incarnate*, Hodder and Stoughton 1977, p. 41.

44. Ibid., p. 23.

45. Tertullian, *Against Praxeas*, chs. 20–22.

46. See J. N. D. Kelly, op. cit., p. 121.

47. John 14.9; Matt. 10.40; Mark 2.1–12; Rom. 14.10 and II Cor. 5.10. The AV of Rom. 14.10 reads 'judgment-seat of Christ', but the manuscript evidence decisively favours 'God' as the correct reading.

48. For Athanasius, see my *The Making of Christian Doctrine*, p. 97; for Barth, see K. Barth, *Church Dogmatics* I/1, T. & T. Clark 1936, p. 340.

49. See 'Christianity without Incarnation?', in *The Myth of God Incarnate*, ed. John Hick, SCM Press 1977, p. 4. For a detailed study of patristic exegesis of the Fourth Gospel, see my *The Spiritual Gospel*, Cambridge University Press 1960.

4. Jesus and the Way of Faith

1. Note how the abrupt form of the Gethsemane prayer ('Abba, Father, all things are possible to thee; remove this cup from me') of Mark 14.36 is toned down in Matt. 26.39 ('My Father, if it be possible . . .') and Luke 22.42 ('Father, if thou art willing . . .').

2. Cf. J. Macquarrie, *The Christian Hope*, Mowbrays 1978, pp. 51–5, 63.

3. See p. 29 above.

4. W. H. Vanstone, *Love's Endeavour, Love's Expense*, Darton, Longman and Todd 1977, p. 65.

5. See pp. 9–11 above.

6. Thomas Aquinas, *Summa Theologiae* 3a, 7,3.

7. Hans Küng, *On Being a Christian*, Collins 1977, p. 581.

8. See *The Remaking of Christian Doctrine*, pp. 62f.

9. R. C. Moberly, *Atonement and Personality*, John Murray 1901, p. 138 (italics original).

10. Op. cit., p. 143.

11. Ibid.

12. Op. cit., pp. 116–33.

13. William Sanday, *The Life of Christ in Recent Research*, Oxford University Press 1907, pp. 248f.

14. Op. cit., p. 246.

15. Op. cit., p. 248.

16. H. Rashdall, 'Dr Moberly's Theory of the Atonement', *JTS*, Vol. III, 1902, pp. 178–211.

17. Art. cit., p. 210.

18. See F. W. Dillistone, *The Christian Understanding of the Atonement*, Methuen 1967, p. 28 n.18.

19. See p. 58 above.

20. Matt. 13.13. Note Matthew's alteration of the 'so that' of Mark 4.12 to 'because'.

21. E. Linnemann, *Parables of Jesus*, SPCK 1966, p. 41.

22. Op. cit., pp. 30f.

23. See p. 61 above.

24. See e.g. John 9.40f.; Mark 3.28–30. For the Christian significance of the denunciation of the Pharisees, see pp. 81, 84 below.

25. Cf. C. R. Driver in *The Guardian*, 17 March 1966, cited by V. de Waal, *What is the Church?*, SCM Press 1969: 'The church, of course, has always deeply distrusted Jesus' reprehensible affection for parables. Its instinct . . . has always been to lay the "truth" on the line and turn up the volume . . . But as any serious artist knows, the truth then ceases to be the truth.'

26. Anselm, *Cur Deus Homo* I, 21.

27. Ibid., 2,22.

5. The Church and the Purpose of God

1. See pp. 43–6 above.

2. See pp. 39–43 above.

3. *Singulari Quadam*, Denzinger 1647. Cited by H. R. Schlette, *Towards a Theology of Religions*, Burns and Oates 1966, p. 16.

4. *De Necessitate Ecclesiae ad Salutem* (1949: Denziger 3866–73), condemning the views of Leonard Feeney.

5. W. H. Vanstone, op. cit., pp. 25f.

6. C. Davis, *A Question of Conscience*, Hodder and Stoughton 1967, p. 220.

7. K. Rahner, *Foundations of Christian Faith*, Darton, Longman and Todd 1978, pp. 142f.

8. K. Rahner, op. cit., p. 323.

9. Jeremias, for example, thinks that the reference to Jeremiah 31.31–34 in the last supper saying 'shows the beginning of theological reflection', while nonetheless regarding it as 'highly probable that Jesus declared that the time for the New Covenant had come' (J. Jeremias, *The Eucharistic Words of Jesus*, Blackwell 1955, pp. 128, 135).

10. See E. P. Sanders, *Paul and Palestinian Judaism*, SCM Press 1977, pp. 11f.

11. S. Weil, *First and Last Notebooks*, Oxford University Press 1970, p. 298.

12. H. R. Niebuhr, *The Responsible Self*, Harper and Row 1963, p. 22.

13. See my 'Ignatius and Church Order', to appear in *Studia Patristica*, Pergamon Press 1982.

14. Ignatius, *Magnesians* 6,1; *Trallians* 3,1.

15. The primary architects of this development were Hegesippus and Irenaeus. See W. Telfer, *The Office of a Bishop*, Darton, Longman and Todd 1962, pp. 107–20, and H. von Campenhausen, *Ecclesiastical Authority and Spiritual Power in the Church of the First Three Centuries*, A. & C. Black 1969, pp. 163–9.

16. The process described does not begin with Ignatius, but can be seen already in the Pastoral Epistles. See J. L. Houlden, 'The Idea of the Church', in *Theological Explorations 3*, SCM Press 1978, p. 57, for a balanced assessment of the need for, but also the loss involved in, the developments reflected in the first epistle to Timothy with its 'anxious concern to establish proper organs of authority'. 'Law (I Tim. 1.8) has reappeared as unambiguous good and it is hard to avoid the sense that in many essential respects Christianity is Judaism transposed into another key.'

17. C. Davis, op. cit., pp. 198f. See also my *What is Theology?*, pp. 94f. Cf. also the remark of E. Schillebeeckx, *Ministry*, SCM Press 1981, p. 75: 'With a shift in the dominant picture of man and the world, with social and economic changes and a new social and cultural sensibility and set of emotions, a church order which has grown up through history can in fact hinder and obstruct precisely what in earlier times it was intended to ensure: the building up of a Christian community.' The argument which is expressed here, following Charles Davis, in terms of the hierarchical character of the ministry, applies with equal force to its exclusively male character.

18. F. J. A. Hort, *Christian Ecclesia*, Macmillan 1897, p. 291.

19. Hort, op. cit., p. 290.

20. See p. 61 above.

21. Vanstone, op. cit., pp. 98f. Vanstone's account would seem to call for some modification, since there are other places, e.g. within Judaism, where the creative love of God is recognized as love.

22. Karl Rahner, 'The Christian and the Future', in *Herder Correspondence*, July 1965, p. 208, cited by V. de Waal, *What is the Church?*, p. 63. Cf. the remark of H. R. Niebuhr in terms of sonship. 'By Jesus Christ men are empowered to become sons of God – not as those who are saved out of a perishing world but as those who know that the world is being saved.'

23. See pp. 27–8 above.

24. Rahner, art. cit., p. 209.

25. C. Davis, op. cit., pp. 222, 224.

26. J. Drury, *The Pot and the Knife*, SCM Press 1979, p. 84.

6. Worship and Action

1. See Shepherd of Hermas, *Vis.* 2,4,1 and 3,11,1–3.

2. See G. Wainwright, 'Recent Eucharistic Revision', in *The Study of Liturgy*, ed. C. Jones, G. Wainwright, E. Yarnold, SPCK 1978, p. 287.

3. E. C. Ratcliff, 'Post-Reformation Worship', in *Worship and Education* (Report of a Conference convened by the National Society), SPCK 1939,

p. 21. The quotation within the quotation is from Edward Thompson, *Night Falls on Shiva's Hill*, ch. 7.

4. See p. 18 above.

5. J. L. Houlden, 'Liturgy and her Companions: A Theological Appraisal', in *Explorations in Theology 3*, SCM Press 1978, p. 91.

6. Ibid., p. 89.

7. See p. 24 above.

8. See pp. 61–5 above.

9. See *The Remaking of Christian Doctrine*, pp. 75–7.

10. G. W. H. Lampe, *God as Spirit*, Oxford University Press 1977, p. 166.

11. See Chapter 3 above.

12. See Ch. 5, n. 9, p. 137.

13. See pp. 91–2 above.

14. See p. 39 above. See also my 'Eucharistic Theology – The Value of Diversity', *Explorations in Theology 4*, pp. 83–90.

15. J. Burnaby, 'Christian Prayer', in *Soundings*, ed. A. R. Vidler, Cambridge University Press 1962, p. 236. Cf. also the similar criticisms of the Book of Common Prayer by Geoffrey Lampe, cited on p. 7 above.

16. *Seikyō Times*, No. 186 (December 1976), p. 3.

17. H. H. Farmer, *The World and God*, London 1935, p. 129. Farmer's view follows F. Heiler, *Prayer*, Oxford University Press 1932, p. 17.

18. See pp. 14–15 above; *The Remaking of Christian Doctrine*, pp. 36–9.

19. See pp. 27–9 above.

20. J. Burnaby, op. cit., pp. 232f.

21. Cf. *The Remaking of Christian Doctrine*, pp. 96–8.

22. See Ch. 4, n. 1, p. 136.

23. Burnaby, op. cit., p. 234.

24. The question has been debated from the earliest days of the church; many of the earliest interpreters (e.g. Tertullian, *On Prayer*, 6; Cyprian, *On the Lord's Prayer*, 18) acknowledge both a literal and a spiritual meaning. Jeremias (*The Prayers of Jesus*, SCM Press 1967, p. 102) in similar vein asserts that 'the petition asks for bread in the fullest sense'; 'it includes "daily bread", but it does not content itself with that'.

25. See *The Remaking of Christian Doctrine*, p. 100, and the references to W. G. Maclagan, *The Theological Frontier of Ethics*, there.

26. Burnaby, op. cit., p. 233.

27. Ibid.

28. P. R. Baelz, *Prayer and Providence*, SCM Press 1968, p. 118.

29. In this part of the discussion, I am indebted to an unpublished MPhil thesis of the University of London by Christopher Hill, entitled 'Intercession in the Light of Modern Theology.'

30. See p. 46 above.

31. See p. 91 above.

32. J. M. Gustafson, *Protestant and Roman Catholic Ethics*, SCM Press 1979, pp. 37f.

33. David Jenkins, 'The Concept of the Human', in *Technology and Social Justice*, ed. R. H. Preston, SCM Press 1971, p. 216. Jenkins also speaks of 'the *rhetoric* of values, aims and talk of "the human" ' (ibid., p. 211: my italics).

34. H. P. Owen, 'Some Philosophical Problems in Christian Ethics', *Theology* LXXVI, January 1973, p. 16, reprinted in *Duty and Discernment*, ed. G. R. Dunstan, SCM Press 1975, p. 2.

35. P. R. Baelz, *Christian Obedience in a Permissive Context*, Athlone Press 1973, p. 8.

36. See P. H. Nowell-Smith, 'Morality: Religious and Secular', in *Christian Ethics and Contemporary Philosophy*, ed. I. T. Ramsey, SCM Press 1966, pp. 95–112.

37. See my *What is Theology?*, p. 74.

38. I. T. Ramsey, 'Moral Judgments and God's Commands', in *Christian Ethics and Contemporary Philosophy*, p. 152.

39. N. H. Snaith, *The Distinctive Ideas of the Old Testament*, Epworth Press 1944, p. 60.

40. G. E. Hughes, 'A Christian Basis for Ethics', *Heythrop Journal* Vol. XIII, January 1972, p. 31 (italics original).

41. H. P. Owen, art. cit., pp. 17f. (*Duty and Discernment*, p. 4: my italics).

42. J. Macquarrie, *Three Issues in Ethics*, SCM Press 1970, p. 90.

43. R. A. McCormick, 'Notes on Moral Theology: April–September 1970', *Theological Studies* 32, March 1971, p. 74 (italics original).

44. Ibid., p. 72 (italics original).

45. Columba Ryan, 'The Traditional Concept of Natural Law', in *Light on the Natural Law*, ed. Illtud Evans, Burns and Oates 1965, p. 20.

46. G. F. Woods, 'Natural Law and Christian Ethics', *Theology* LXVIII, June 1965, p. 276 (reprinted in *Duty and Discernment*, p. 39).

47. See Charles Curran, *Catholic Moral Theology in Dialogue*, Fides Publishers 1972, pp. 21f.; Enda McDonagh, 'A Comment from the Roman Catholic Tradition', *Duty and Discernment*, p. 50.

48. Richard A. McCormick, 'Human Significance and Christian Significance', in *Norm and Context in Christian Ethics*, ed. G. H. Outka and Paul Ramsey, SCM Press 1968, p. 247.

49. The contrast between an old static view of human nature and a modern dynamic one must not be overdrawn. Thomas Aquinas, for example, recognizes that 'the just and the good . . . are formally and everywhere the same, because the principles of right in natural reason do not change . . . Taken in the material sense, they are not the same everywhere and for all men, and this is so by reason of the mutability of man's nature and the diverse conditions in which men and things find themselves in different environments and times' (*De Malo* 2,4 and 13: cited by L. Dupré, 'Situation Ethics and Objective Morality', *Theological Studies* 28, June 1967, p. 251).

50. Columba Ryan, art. cit., p. 32.

51. See pp. 18–22 above.

52. C. Davis, *Theology and Political Society*, Cambridge University Press 1980, p. 152.

53. S. Crites, 'Myth, Story, History', in *Parable, Myth and Language*, ed. T. Stoneburner, Church Society for College Work 1968, p. 68.

54. R. W. Hepburn, 'Vision and Choice in Morality', in *Christian Ethics and Contemporary Philosophy*, pp. 181–95.

55. Iris Murdoch, ibid., p. 211.

56. See Chapter 5 above.

57. Daniel Jenkins, 'Faith and Politics in Britain Today', in *Christian Faith and Political Hopes*, ed. H. Willmer, Epworth Press 1979, p. 67.

58. Cf. John Taylor, *The Go-Between God*, SCM Press 1972, p. 147. 'If the Christian contribution is not being given in the arena of race conflict or housing or Third World development, we may blame Christians for not doing it, we may blame "the church" for not teaching them to do it, but we should not blame "the church" for not doing it.'

59. Cf. my *The Christian Fathers*, Hodder and Stoughton 1966, reissued SCM Press 1977, pp. 138–40.

7. *God as Spirit*

1. G. W. H. Lampe, *God as Spirit*, Oxford University Press 1977.

2. Ibid., p. 288.

3. See p. 24 above.

4. For patristic commentators see my *The Divine Apostle*, Cambridge University Press 1967, pp. 30–7; for modern commentators see Marie Isaacs, *The Concept of Spirit*, Heythrop Monographs 1976, pp. 70–81.

5. K. Rahner, *Foundations of Christian Faith*, Darton, Longman and Todd 1978, p. 32.

6. S. Kierkegaard, *Sickness unto Death*, Oxford University Press 1941, p. 17. The quotation continues with some increasingly complex qualifications: '. . . or it is that in the relation (which accounts for it) that the relation relates itself to its own self; the self is not the relation but (consists in the fact) that the relation relates itself to its own self'.

7. John Taylor, *The Go-Between God*, SCM Press 1972, p. 8.

8. G. W. H. Lampe, op. cit., p. 50.

9. John Taylor, op. cit., pp. 5f.

10. See my 'Holy Spirit in Christian Theology', *Theology* LXVI, June 1963, pp. 233–7, reprinted in *Explorations in Theology* 4, SCM Press 1979, pp. 67–72.

11. See P. Tillich, *Systematic Theology*, Vol. 3, Nisbet 1964, p. 118.

12. G. Marcel, *The Mystery of Being*, Vol. I, Harvill 1950, p. 205 (italics original).

13. Ibid., pp. 208f.

14. Ibid., Vol. II, Harvill 1951, p. 45.

15. See pp. 9–11 above. Leslie Dewart indeed speaks of it as 'the only valid "proof" for the "existence" of God that I know of', a phrase closely parallel to that of Ogden quoted on p. 11 above (see *The Future of Belief*, Burns and Oates 1966, p. 177).

16. P. Prini, *Gabriel Marcel e la metodologia dell'inverificabile*, Editrice Studium 1950, p. 7.

17. Ibid., p. 123. These references to Prini are cited by Joe McCown, *Availability: Gabriel Marcel and the Phenomenology of Human Openness*, AAR Studies in Religion 14, Scholars Press 1978, pp. 50f.

18. Dewart, op. cit., pp. 173–85.

19. See p. 29 above.

20. Lampe, op. cit., p. 144.

21. Ibid., pp. 12f. See also my 'The Holy Spirit and the Incarnation', in *The Holy Spirit*, ed. D. Kirkpatrick, Tidings 1974, pp. 90–103, which was much indebted to Professor Lampe's earlier article 'The Holy Spirit and the Person of Christ', in *Christ, Faith and History*, ed. S. W. Sykes and J. P. Clayton, Cambridge University Press 1972, pp. 111–30.

22. See p. 87 above.

23. See Shakespeare, *Henry IV, Part I*, Act 3, Scene 1, 53–5.

24. See pp. 93–103 above. Cf. also my essay in *Christian Believing. A Report by the Doctrine Commission of the Church of England*, SPCK 1974, pp. 125–32.

25. Augustine, *De Spiritu et Litera* XXXIV, 60.

INDEX OF NAMES

INDEX OF SUBJECTS

Index of Subjects